CONVERSATIONS WITH AN EAGLE

CONVERSATIONS

Brenda Cox

the story of a
remarkable
relationship

WITH AN **EAGLE**

GREYSTONE BOOKS

Douglas & McIntyre Publishing Group

Vancouver / Toronto

02 03 04 05 06   5 4 3 2 1

Greystone Books
A division of Douglas & McIntyre Ltd.
2323 Quebec Street, Suite 201
Vancouver, British Columbia
Canada V5T 4S7
www.greystonebooks.com

National Library of Canada Cataloguing in Publication Data
Cox, Brenda, 1967–
    Conversations with an eagle

    ISBN 1-55054-811-5

    1. Bald eagle. 2. Ichabod (Eagle). 3. Human-animal relationships. I. Title.
QL696.F32C69 2002   598.9'43   C2002-910389-4

Cover and text design by Peter Cocking
Typesetting by Rhonda Ganz
Front cover photograph: Swift/Vanuga Images/Corbis
Back cover photograph: Jo-Anne Clark
Printed and bound in Canada by Friesens

Greystone Books is committed to reducing the consumption of old-
growth forests in the books it publishes. This book is one step towards
that goal. It is printed on acid-free paper that is 100% ancient-forest-
free, and it has been processed chlorine-free.

We gratefully acknowledge the financial support of the Canada Council
for the Arts, the British Columbia Ministry of Tourism, Small Business and
Culture, and the Government of Canada through the Book Publishing
Industry Development Program (BPIDP) for our publishing activities.

To all the dedicated volunteers who work with wild birds and

animals, and to Moon Dog, my precious old friend

CONTENTS

There are people who do not know who they are

until they catch their reflection in an eye other than human.

LOREN C. EISELEY

NOTHING IN THE WORLD prepares you for an eagle
leaping to your arm.

Ichabod's head cocked sideways, her eyes sharpened,
then she half leapt, half flew to my outstretched arm. She
curled her talons around the heavy leather glove and lowered her beak to worry the thumb. My arm and hand
belonged to her. That was what she did best: own things.
For eight years, this eagle owned me.

THE MOST REMARKABLE relationship of my life
began on July 25, 1992, at a wildlife sanctuary where
I was a volunteer supervisor. I was twenty-five at the
time. Ichabod, a juvenile bald eagle, was three months
old. I was drawn to her immediately, and until her death
in September 2000, our lives were closely intertwined.
This book is a record of our time together, and a tribute
to the magnificence of bald eagles everywhere.

MEETING ICHABOD

MY EYES WERE CLOSED. That was one luxury of bus travel. I'd been in transit since 7:00 A.M., travelling for an hour and a half from my basement apartment in Coquitlam through Burnaby, New Westminster, Surrey and Delta. I'd run the gamut of cities in British Columbia's Lower Mainland. It was a Saturday morning in July, and I was on my way to O.W.L., the wildlife rehabilitation centre where I volunteered on weekends.

As I sensed the bus moving onto Highway 10, the Ladner Trunk Road, I opened my eyes to flat land that had to work hard to keep the hazy-blue mountains at bay.

My face relaxed. I was out of the city at last. The land stretched before me, and as the bus mounted an overpass, I could see the rind of the shoreline at Boundary Bay. Sometimes I checked the tide charts on TV before I left home, though I hadn't today. The tide was coming in, I speculated. The milk-chocolate mud flats followed a curve that seemed to mimic the shoreline, and I imagined the grey-blue water hungrily creeping towards shore. Flat land and water: two worlds that allowed some peace for a former Prairie woman. Even though I'd lived on the West Coast for four years, the mountains still made me claustrophobic.

I always sat at the front of the bus so I could see out the windshield, but now movement outside the side window caught my eye. A male northern harrier, a marsh hawk, flew parallel to the bus. I scanned the field for a brown-and-rust female. Seeing none, I fixed my gaze on the pewter-coloured male. He was flying beneath the level of the window, and the unusual vantage point let me see him from above as he flew. The hawk's eyes were trained on the ground, no doubt in search of his favourite food. His light-grey plumage seemed ethereal against the tall yellow grasses. After a minute, the bird veered from his course to head across the field, flying low in a repeating flap, flap, glide pattern. My stop was fast approaching. I collected my bag and stood, the bus slowing in response to my movement.

After crossing the busy highway, I stood still for a
moment and breathed in the salt-laden air. A breeze
coming off the water advertised the ocean's powerful presence, though from where I stood I could see only a long,
straight road lined with tall poplars. Except for the air,
I could have been standing on a farmer's road in
Manitoba.

It was a mile and a half from here to the wildlife centre, a route I'd come to know well. As I passed the turn-
off for an abandoned airport, I could see cracked concrete
roads and old runways. I'd explored the area briefly in
the past, and I knew old building foundations crumbled
alongside the roads. I fantasized that pilots had stayed in
these houses with their families during wartime, when
the airport was active.

Once I had crossed the railway line, the poplars gave
way to scrubby blackberry bushes bordering the open
fields of the Boundary Bay Airport, a busy light-plane
facility. On their approaches, planes dropped low over the
road.

As I walked I was accompanied by a great blue heron
that flew just ahead, first landing in the deep ditch beside
the road, then spooking every time I approached him. I
wondered what else would be on my list of birds sighted
today. Herons, red-tailed hawks, harriers, kestrels, snowy
owls, bald eagles, rough-legged hawks, sharp-shinned
hawks and Cooper's hawks were the common diurnal

species. The ditches bordering the road were home to muskrats and mice, and the tall grass around the runways was essential habitat for the single most important prey species, the Townsend's vole.

Sometimes I found it odd to remember I was below sea level, imagining that the rich delta mud beneath the road would become waterlogged and begin to dissolve. But the feeling was offset by my knowledge that, in this bay, the land was actually being added to all the time, as sediment spewed from the mouth of the huge Fraser River was deposited on the shoreline by ocean currents. The fresh- and salt-water mix at the mouth of the Fraser, a few miles away, contributed to the incredible biological wealth of the area. The intertidal belt was a feeding and resting place for thousands of migrating and wintering waterfowl, which grazed on the eelgrass and algae of the salt marsh. Crab, abalone and oysters were present in healthy numbers. Salmon depended on the brackish water of the river plume to cushion their transition from fresh water to salt water on both their seaward migration and the return journey to their birthplace. I wondered if the herring spawn earlier that year had been successful and if the numbers of black brants arriving from Russia had been high.

A glance at my watch told me it was just after nine. I picked up my pace. I was supposed to open the centre as close to nine o'clock as I could manage.

THE INITIALS O.W. L. stood for Orphaned Wild Life. The centre took in orphaned or injured raptors, caring for them and then releasing them back into the wild whenever possible. Over the three years I'd been there the centre had grown from a facility based in the back rooms of a large house, with several banks of outdoor cages, to a large, modern building with many interior sections and a variety of different-sized cages in the back field beyond.

The birds had to be fully functional before they could be returned to the wild, and sometimes, despite veterinary care, a broken wing would heal without regaining its full range of motion. Broken legs and trauma to the brain that affected coordination in even a minor way were also conditions that could result in a non-releasable label. Young birds that had been socialized to people, or "imprinted," might also fall into the non-releasable category, depending on a number of variables: how long they had been exposed to people, how old they were when first contact occurred, and so on. Non-releasable birds were used for educational programs or housed in display cages that could be viewed by the public on guided tours.

The majority of O.W. L. volunteers were interested in working directly with the birds. People just starting out were paired with experienced volunteers to learn about feeding, cleaning cages, and ultimately handling and medicating injured birds of prey. All volunteers were supposed to be over the age of fourteen, although occa-

sionally someone younger was accepted if accompanied
by a parent.

Some volunteers worked with the birds for a period
of time, then moved into the educational area, where they
were trained to give tours, speak to the public at different
venues and help with the popular school program that
took place in a small classroom on O.W.L. property. Office
help was another area for volunteers, as was cage building. Employment Insurance "top-up" programs, in
which E.I. paid unemployed people to work at O.W.L.,
were another source of staffing for the centre. Fishers
often worked at O.W.L. in the off-season.

Part-time staff members were responsible for training
volunteers and overseeing their work. Public tours took
place on weekends, and the number of volunteers required on those days was between four and eight, especially if many of O.W.L.'s patients required intensive care
at the time. Weekdays were quieter, though most school
tours occurred then.

O.W.L. was located on a property in rural Delta. At
first, the centre operated out of the director's house. The
back bedrooms were bird rooms, and a small bank of outside cages served as outdoor containment. Sometimes
medications were given in the dining room or the
kitchen. Gradually, more outside cages were built, and
through the help of grants and donations O.W.L. was
able to build a large care centre to house the birds. Office

space, a lunch room, and various rooms and cages for recuperating birds were contained in the main building. Out back were more cages, including several large, free-standing banks of them.

Two of the centre's most popular educational birds were Lucy, the red-tailed hawk, and Oddey, the handi-capped barn owl. Lucy had a breathing problem thought to originate from pesticides. Oddey had been affected as an embryo by a dose of digitalis; it probably came from his mother ingesting a mouse that had eaten foxglove, a plant rich in the chemical. Both birds were calm around people.

Some weekend mornings I'd ready kennel cabs—dog crates—for Lucy and Oddey and then, with several volunteers, take O.W.L.'s old converted ambulance to an environmental fair. We'd set up tables to display informa-tion about the centre and sell O.W.L. T-shirts, key chains and baseball hats. Two shoulder-height perches stood behind the tables, with Lucy perched on one, Oddey on the other. The birds wore jesses, or leather straps, around their legs, and these were attached to leashes that were tied to the mobile perches. Forprotection, we wore gloves when handling the birds.

Oddey, imprinted strongly to people, often expressed an intense liking or dislike for someone. He seemed to respond particularly to hair colour; he liked most blondes but was choosy about brunettes. (He had been raised by the centre's director, a blonde.) Because the public couldn't approach the birds closely at the fairs, it was at the care centre that Oddey's preferences were most apparent. He preferred women to men and would mount unsuspecting women's heads when they entered his cage. Sometimes he was given the run of the large interim care room while volunteers went about their business. Female volunteers would distract the owl or hold his jesses when men had to pass through the room. Like most barn owls, Oddey had a great fondness for enclosed spaces, and we constructed elaborate cities for him of boxes with towels draped over them. Oddey would often emit little chittering sounds over his food, grooming his dead mice when he wasn't hungry.

Lucy was more standoffish than Oddey. She was well socialized to people but did not consider them her mates. Once you'd earned her trust, however, she relaxed calmly on the glove, gazing at the world around her with brown eyes that looked wise. She had a sense of humour and would play games with the volunteers trying to attach a leash to her jesses or place her in a kennel cab. Despite Oddey's entertaining nature, I found myself more drawn to Lucy. I was always attracted to the birds that were sight oriented. Owls primarily used their hearing to help them locate food in the dark. I found them interesting, but my attention was always pulled to birds that looked into the far distance, seeing things I could only guess at

with their acute vision. Eagles fascinated me. I'd spend
long minutes watching them stare into space with a look
I'd occasionally seen on the faces of aristocratic horses.
In the horse world, in fact, this countenance, ascribed to
fleet thoroughbred racehorses, is known as the "look of
the eagles."

SATURDAY WAS a busy day at O.W.L. After checking
that I had enough volunteers to do both maintenance and
treatment of the resident birds and public tours, I read
the erasable wall charts, looking for new patients or birds
that had been moved to a different location in the centre.

I went first to intensive care, a room with easily accessible smaller cages for the birds needing the most attention. Noting which cages held birds, I dropped curtains
over the doors of these cages, to keep the birds' view of
me to a minimum. I knew that the sight of humans
caused the birds great distress; and anything affecting
their stress levels could hamper their recovery. There
were several young barn owls under scrutiny and an adult
barn owl recently brought in from a local farm. I looked
at the case sheets, noting that none of the owls were
on medication. The baby owls were still partly clothed
in soft down, I noticed as I lifted the curtain and peeked
in quickly through the wire-and-dowel window. The
beginnings of black-flecked, butterscotch-coloured feathers were visible through the fluffy white baby feathers. As

I left the room, I heard characteristic defensive hissing from the youngsters.

Next I walked through a set of swinging doors into interim care, where the cages were small rooms, allowing the birds more freedom of movement. Each interim room had a large window that looked out onto the hall. These windows were covered with square-gauge wire; dowelling was set vertically in the sill, preventing the birds from contacting the wire. When the centre was busy with volunteers, these windows too were covered with sheets, allowing the nervous birds a respite. The wall charts that hung from each cage door contained information on the bird's date of arrival, its species, the nature of its injury, any medication being administered and feeding instructions. A plastic sleeve on each door also held a more detailed case sheet.

As I approached the door to one cage, I heard the loud crackling of large feathers being lifted and settled against a body. The noise was like the rustling of a stiff petticoat. Even before I looked at the chart, I knew that behind the covered window was a bald eagle. The sound of its big wings shifting, then flapping against the air, was unmistakable.

I looked briefly at the bird's case sheet. She was female, approximately twelve weeks old. She'd been brought in on Wednesday. I made a mental note to check the food logs to make sure she was eating. New admissions sometimes refused to eat because of the strange new environment and the unfamiliar food.

I lifted a corner of the curtain covering the large glass-less window. Framed by wooden bars, a juvenile eagle jerked her head forward, eyes locked on me. The piercing stare eagles normally exhibit was replaced in this case by a curious expression. I was startled, then intrigued, by the bird's friendly gaze. But it disturbed me, too. An eagle of this age should be suspicious of people, I thought.

Despite her formidable size, the eagle was rangy and leggy, giving the impression that preteen girls often give of potential mixed with awkwardness. It always surprised me to see how juvenile eagles were as large in height as an adult. This bird was feathered completely in glossy dark brown and had eyes to match. The striking yellow eyes and the dramatic white head and tail characteristic of the bald eagle adult would not even begin to emerge until her third or fourth year.

I let the curtain drop and returned to studying the sheet in my hand. I wanted to know where the eagle had come from. Carrying the sheet, I went back through the swinging doors to the front of the care centre. The medical room had a file system that listed birds by their case number. I looked at the paper in my hand: 92-119. The eagle was the 119th raptor of 1992. I pulled her card from the files, recognizing the neat upright printing of the Wednesday supervisor. The eagle had been found in the Heffley Creek area of B.C. near Kamloops on June 20, I read. After almost four weeks at Kamloops Wildlife Park, she'd been driven to O.W.L. by one of the park's directors. The new resident was housed at O.W.L. in an indoor cage that measured ten feet by ten feet. Sliding doors allowed volunteers to provide the eagle with an escape route into an adjoining cage when a major cage cleaning was required.

I set the eagle's food, a large dead quail, on a nearby counter. Food records indicated that she had been eating in captivity. Once I got back to her cage, I looked again at her case sheet. "Abnormal" was checked off in reference to the bird's legs and feet. Her legs were characterized as "swollen and hot to the touch" when she first arrived, and subsequent X-rays showed a small fracture, called a greenstick, in her left leg. Suspicious of bone problems relating to diet, the centre's staff had sent blood samples to a lab for testing. If the results indicated a calcium and an iron deficiency, two deficiencies that often go hand in hand, then the bird would be given supplements.

Stapled to the case sheet was a page outlining what was known about the bird's history.

June 20/92: from Central Valley Animal Hospital, Kamloops
· young and weak, all else O.K.
· nest fell out of tree during high winds in Heffley Creek area

- hand-fed cut-up chicks, approx. 4, and few beef
  chunks daily (2 × a day)
- deloused with powder

July 14/92
- perching
- eating on own, approx. 4–6 chicks and beef chunks
  and add piece of fish

Reading this, I suspected a calcium deficiency myself.
Raptors, especially juveniles, need the bones and internal organs of their prey to provide adequately for their
nutritional needs. Even during the short time this eagle
had been in captivity, her diet could have adversely
affected her bones.

With each new patient, the volunteers at O.W. L.
assigned a pronoun. But determining the sex of an eagle
is not straightforward. There are no plumage or coloura-
tion differences between males and females. Technology
offers two methods: taking an ultrasound to reveal
testes or ovaries, or testing the DNA of flesh on the end
of a feather. Some people advocate measuring beak
depth; on bald eagles, a deeper beak indicates a female.
Others consider the hallux, the backward-facing toe
and talon on an eagle's foot, to be an indicator of gender.
The talon on the female bird is larger and longer. Female
eagles are generally larger than males, too. As with so
many other birds and animals, an eagle's size is also

linked to location. In the Interior of British Columbia, the eagles are smaller than those on the coast. The northern birds are the largest of all.

The largest eagle I had ever seen was a female from Haida Gwaii, the Queen Charlotte Islands. A volunteer had noticed the bird's wings tipping the partitions between cages in the outdoor eagle pens. Since the space between partitions was more than eight feet, we knew we were looking at a very large bird. Before she was released, we measured her wingspan at nine feet.

The new juvenile eagle weighed 11.9 pounds. Since their bones are hollow, eagles are much less substantial than they look. The average male eagle weighs from seven to nine pounds, and females usually tip the scales at somewhere between ten and thirteen pounds.

The hallux of this young eagle was longer then most of the birds considered male at O.W. L., and her beak had more depth. It was not crucial to be accurate about the sex of the bird being rehabilitated, since the centre was not in the business of breeding birds. An educated guess had been made, and the juvenile was marked down as female.

Volunteers had already given her a name, too. According to the other Saturday supervisor, the young eagle sometimes showed a submissive posture when people approached, hanging her head as if it weighed heavily on her neck. This had reminded the volunteers of Ichabod

Crane, the main character in the recent movie version of *The Legend of Sleepy Hollow.* Volunteers began referring to the young bird as Ichabod, and the name stuck.

I replaced the case sheet in the holder on the door. Drawing back the edge of the curtain covering the wood-barred window, I again peeked in. I was "room service," and I felt I should locate the young eagle before opening the door of her cage.

Hunkered down in the corner, Ichabod looked lost and preoccupied. I grabbed her food, crouched, opened the door and crab-walked in. This method had proven, in my experience, the best approach to confined, nervous birds of prey. I had to reach the stump by the door and place the dead quail there before retreating. I kept my eyes low, glancing over occasionally at the bird's feet to see where she was but avoiding meeting her eyes.

A rustling sound startled me. I raised my eyes and turned my head as I withdrew my hand from the stump.

Ichabod stood on the floor, two feet away.

I continued my crablike retreat, backing up with my face averted.

The bird did not appear on the stump, and I smelled a faint, rotten smell close by. Perplexed, I turned my head again.

My eyeball was inches from hers.

She gazed at me without the typical reticence of a wild creature. Her head feathers were smooth, her expression calm. I crouched there, very still, looking into eyes that could see a fish from a mile in the sky. I felt a frisson run through me.

Before I could move, Ichabod turned away and sidled, with the drunken swagger typical of eagles, to her dinner. Deliberately, as if she found its wholeness distasteful, she lifted the quail from the stump with her beak, then retired to her corner, the food swaying from side to side.

I backed out of the cage and closed the door. Breathing deeply, I looked down to see my hands shaking with adrenalin.

I knew what the eagle had felt was curiosity: what was that tall creature doing down there? As for me, for a moment, I had caught my reflection in her potent bronze eyes.

I was hooked.

2

THE WORLD OUTSIDE

WILDLIFE HAS always fascinated me.
I grew up in Winnipeg's west end,
minutes from where the Prairie city became country.
Even as a small child, I didn't like to be inside buildings
or under roofs. I wanted the sky above me. Big winds and
long, unbroken views filled me with excitement, as did
moving water and drooping trees.

I remember very clearly my first obsession with a bird.
I was four years old. Sitting in dewy grass in the small
back yard of our L-shaped rancher, I could feel the seat
of my cords growing damp. I didn't find the seeping wet-
ness unpleasant, just another of the world's interesting

sensations. I had been pulling up grass, and my fingers were tinged with green. As I got ready to uproot the next clump, I saw before me the most amazing bird. Its tail was longer than its body, and the deep iridescent green of its back gleamed in the sun. With its black head, shoulders and chest and the snowy plumage above and below its wings, it seemed to be a fantasy bird.

Our screen door banged suddenly, and the fairytale bird took to the air. It teetered for a moment on the fence, the wand of its tail lifting and dropping as it paused on the outermost edge of my world. Then it stepped off the fence, opened its wings and disappeared. I turned in rage to see who had driven the bird away, but there was no one there. The door swung back and forth a few times before closing again with a decisive slam.

I looked stubbornly for the magpie after that, but I never saw it again. Even after I had started school, I would watch for the bird from the back seat of the car or from my classroom window. I saw a jewelled flash several times, but it turned out to be only light glinting off a piece of metal. In the meantime, though, I began to pay attention to the other creatures of the natural world, eagerly noting the flicker of movement in the tall yellow grass that heralded the approach of a coyote or the raunchy rolling walk of a crow. When I pointed out a woodpecker drumming a dead snag behind the school to my classmates, they laughed, asking if I was a "bush girl."

My family's summer cabin at Big Whiteshell Lake in southeastern Manitoba became the best place to indulge my intense fascination with nature. I was two when my father built the cabin, and our family camped in a tent in the framed skeleton of the building for the first season.

Our cabin perched four hundred feet above the lake on a giant rock. It was painted "Navaho red," as was the dock. The rust-coloured paint came off on our damp hands. The cabin was raised a foot and a half above the ground by concrete blocks, and the mysterious crawl space below housed a myriad of imaginary creatures ready to grab me at night as I ran up the stairs to the door.

One of my dad's first rituals on arrival was to remove the plywood shutters covering the cabin's big front windows. I would stand inside, waiting excitedly for the view to be revealed. As each piece of plywood vibrated, then dropped miraculously from the window, balanced carefully above my dad's head, a different piece of lake and sky would appear. The sky was like something the lake had dreamed up, its hues mirrored by the reflecting pane of water. Stepping around me, my mom would sweep up the dead ants that stippled the linoleum.

Chores like unpacking I avoided. As soon as I'd thrown my bag on the upper bunk of the bed I shared with my sister, I'd run from the cabin through a screen of trees, heading for the front of the cliff the cabin sat on. My eyes would travel over the rock's familiar contours

and, half sliding, half walking, I'd make my way down
to a hollow scooped out of the rock face. As I sat, keeping
very still, the world around me would return to the
rhythm I had disturbed. A song sparrow would resume
its liquid warble; a woodpecker would go back to drilling
the nearby poplar tree. I arranged pen and paper around
me, along with favourite books like Sid Marty's *Men for
the Mountains,* a story about the exploits of a park ranger.
I followed tiny sparrows through my binoculars, watching the intimate intricacies of a bird's life. I wrote poems,
drew pictures and absorbed the fragrant spice of Jack
pine needles and lake breezes.

I loved Winnipeg winters, too, despite temperatures
that could drop as low as -37°C. My dad was an avid
cross-country skier, and he'd often cajole my mom into
a family outing in the nearby Assiniboine forest. He'd lay
our skis upside down across a sawhorse, then check the
TV channel that showed the weather to find out how
cold it was so he'd know which kind of wax to apply.
My mom would stuff us into our warm clothes, and then
we'd head for the park. Skis clamped to boots, pole han-
dles looped over mittens, we'd ski through the gate, my
sister and I whacking our skis on exposed rocks while
my impatient father skied on ahead.

We'd use the smooth sweep of his tracks as a guide.
I wanted to be graceful like he was, to enter a rhythm
as I cleaved the clean, cold air, flowing over the hidden
earth on a soft snow blanket.

Shortly after I started high school, I began to do chores at a stable in exchange for riding privileges. Soon I was spending every extra moment there, escaping the social pressures of school for the old wood barn and the feeling of a pitchfork in my hand. Riding out from the stable on a red bay mare named Java, I'd head for the forest, travelling along the edges of a farmer's field. I discovered that, on horseback, I could approach animals like deer, foxes and grouse, which were too nervous to allow me to get near them on foot. I felt like a centaur, a blend of horse and girl. The land seemed to embrace Java and me, so that we were not foreigners on the forest soil but native species.

Winter rides were quiet, with few other riders braving the cold. I imagined, in the giant snowy womb of the forest, that Java and I walked where humans had never trod. I'd look back over my shoulder at the soft collapsed holes that signalled our path. Alongside but less obvious were the tiny fork tracks of birds and the delicate tracery of small branches that had sprung up through the cushion of snow. Thin grey shadows took shape, then faded, as deer picked their way through the dense foliage. Whenever I spotted one, I'd freeze in position, the way I saw the deer themselves do. Java, responding to my tightened muscles, would stop too, her gentle exhalations forming small clouds. I'd hold my breath until the deer had slipped into the undergrowth, afraid of upsetting the delicate balance that kept the animal from spooking.

When it melted from sight, I'd let out my pent-up breath in a whoosh, causing Java to jump and snort.

Sometimes, instead of going to the forest, Java and I would head across the flat reaches of land to the farmer's road bisecting the field. We'd walk first to warm up, trot briefly, then break into a gallop as the horse's hooves touched the dirt road. She loved the routine, and any deviation was met with resistance. I lay over her neck as she bit into the ground with her hooves, propelling us through the air with astonishing power. After she slowed, I'd find my breath coming in gasps, as if I had been running alongside.

The stable where I worked was busy in the winter with sleigh rides. I'd mix hot mashes of bran, oats and molasses for the hard-working horses. As I buckled a warm wool rug around the giant body of a Percheron, he'd lift his gleaming head, muzzle dripping with mash, and direct a grateful look my way.

I wrote poems about horses and other animals, finding the same peace in writing that I did in the forest. I finally worked up the nerve to show them to my English teacher. He was very encouraging.

Otherwise, high school was like a foreign land. At lunchtime, I'd seek out quiet places where I could sit and imagine big trees shrouding a trail as I followed the tracks of wolves through dense forest. I would come out of my reverie from time to time to watch the other girls my age as they stood close together, speaking with

22

great animation. I wondered what they talked about, what excited them so much, and sometimes I eavesdropped on their conversations. I envied their close ties. Their hips would bump together as they walked around and around the soccer field, throwing back their heads to release peals of laughter. The boys would burst suddenly from the gym doors, charging the air as they ran out onto the field. The girls' head-tilting would become more affected then, the swing of their hair in the bright sunlight more pronounced. I stood on the edge of the crowd, unsure how to enter.

It was easier to retreat into the world of nature, where it was unimportant what you wore or who you spoke to. Caught up in the movements of a songbird on a branch before me, I could let the rest of the world drift away. Tears would come to my eyes as I watched the giant wings of an owl traverse an air corridor through the trees. The vibrating thrum of a grouse would shake the air around me and cause a lump to form in my throat.

There was one girl who played sports with the boys and walked about the school with the same conviction of her influence. She seemed to crack open a passage in the air and stride through it. She was respected for her physical prowess but on the outside socially. Her name was Renata.

I had first heard of the stable that housed Java from Renata. She worked at the barn in exchange for riding privileges on a big draft-cross horse named Teeac. In her spare time, at her parents' home, she rehabilitated injured birds of prey. Cages in her back yard held a Swainson's hawk and a great grey owl. Basement rooms housed recuperating birds of prey such as snowy owls. Renata's parents seemed to be as interested in birds as she was. She and her mother would often compare notes about the birds they'd sighted that day. Bird books littered the tables and shelves; some lay open, dog-eared and slightly grubby. Bald eagles were uncommon in Manitoba, and my first glimpse of one outside of a zoo was an injured bird sent to Renata from Ontario. She let me peek inside its cage, then closed the door quickly as the bird became agitated. Used to the size of our local hawks, I was awestruck by the big eagle with its gleaming yellow eyes. The great grey owl, Grayl, would ride on her arm as she walked the neighbourhood. A large crow stood on her shoulder while she biked through the streets. Once, when she was invited to our cabin at Big Whiteshell, Renata showed up holding a kestrel, a diminutive falcon, and carrying her clothes in a plastic grocery bag.

One spring day when the fields were still laced with snow, Renata asked me to assist her in capturing an injured bird of prey. We drove out past the floodway and the perimeter highway, the demarcation of city limits for Winnipeg, in search of an injured snowy owl. Renata had heard one was out there. We didn't have our licences, so Renata's dad was our chauffeur. He sat in the car listening to music while we conducted our search.

When Renata approached a solid white blob in the middle of one field, it moved. The chase was on. The snowy owl half ran, half flew. Its hanging right wing skewed its course into a series of large arcs. Despite this handicap, the bird's speed was surprising. One of us chased while the other cut off the owl's trajectory. I ran until my feet were twice their size with thick globby mud. Renata, having much more stamina, finally caught the owl.

Renata had a standing invitation at a local vet clinic to bring in wild birds she had found for X-rays after hours. This time I accompanied her and the owl. Renata indicated that my job was to keep the bird, a female, on her back on the table. I wrapped my hand around the owl's thick, softly feathered legs. After donning what looked like welder's gloves, Renata told me to be certain I had control of the owl's feet, since it was the bird's claws that could do us the most damage.

Examining the feet I held steady, with their sharp, thin black talons and short broad toes, I was enchanted to discover the soft pale-pink pad of skin along the bottom. It was like the skin of a newborn baby, I thought. But my peaceful reverie was cut off as the large owl began to struggle in my hands, her talons clenching, her wings thumping hard against the table. Her beak snapped repeatedly, clacking loudly.

"Cover her head with a towel," Renata instructed.

The bird calmed immediately as her world darkened. I was sad to lose sight of her giant yellow lantern eyes with their inky black pupils. I considered, for a moment, lifting the towel and sneaking a peek. I was tempted to stroke her white chest with its vertical black streaks. But I knew that doing either would increase the bird's stress. So I stood quietly, eyeing the thick body with its Persian cat fluff, the nerve endings of my bare wrist awakened to the soft, shirred fringe of feathers resting gently there. Whenever I shifted my weight or moved my hand slightly, loud clacking and struggling started under the towel. When it was time to move to the X-ray room, I was stiff with the effort of keeping still.

I had never experienced such presence in a living creature. Though stoutly built, weighing in at four pounds, the owl seemed even larger. Occasionally her wings would escape my hold, the towel would slip off, and she'd flap her wings to their full span of four and a half feet, lifting my hair from my face. It was like a science fiction movie in which aliens were experimenting on human beings—except this time, we were the aliens.

I kept up my friendship with Renata, but at fifteen a girl from a different high school caught my interest. I became Toni's shadow, hoping that some of her casual ease with boys would rub off on me. That summer, Toni came to Big Whiteshell Lake with us. The idea of showing someone my special places thrilled me. Under her critical eyes, my pride in my dad's hand-built cabin wavered for a moment. But as I led her around the front of the cabin, placing my feet in the same hollows in the grass and moss that they'd stepped into for years, I could see that Toni was inspired by the sudden view of open water and distant islands.

Before we left Winnipeg, I'd told Toni about the campground at the north end of the lake, where peaceful families mixed with boisterous partiers. As we walked down the steep path towards the water, she was already speculating about when my dad would drive us over there. When we reached the dock, I heard the haunting trill of a loon. I stopped to listen, but Toni didn't seem interested.

The next day my dad agreed to take us to the campground, and within minutes of our being dropped off, Toni had charmed two boys into giving us a ride in their boat. White-capped waves were angling across the north bay. By the time they reached the beach, the big waves had become gentle ripples. The boys' chunky silver boat rested on the sand. As they dragged it into the water, I watched a flotilla of ducks float past the pier and drift towards us. Tiny babies bobbed behind an adult female.

The starting of the boat's old Evinrude motor over-rode the din of families cooking over firepits and the interwoven threads of many types of music. Toni and I sloshed through the water and pulled ourselves over the gunwales. One boy gunned the motor and spun the wheel, creating heaving waves. The ducks had settled in water away from the beach, and the boy steered for them. I opened my mouth to protest, but the wind ripped away my words. The mother duck half flew, half swam out of the way, and I saw the babies scattered on both sides of the bow for an instant as the boat passed over where they'd been. I dove across the boat looking for their little yellow-brown bodies. When the boy turned the boat in a circle for another run, I stood to get his attention and shouted "No!", ignoring the other boy's restraining hand on my arm. The driver looked at me, made a face and swung back near the beach. I scrambled out, barely splashing clear before the boat took off again. Through the watery spray, I caught a glimpse of Toni's billowing green T-shirt and laughing face.

Farther down the beach, I watched the mother duck shepherd her undamaged brood along the shallows. I waited on a bench for Toni's return, alternating between anger and fear of remaining forever outside the social world of teenagers. I was absurdly grateful when she sat down beside me an hour later.

AFTER HIGH SCHOOL, I floated from one part-time job to another. I was rarely happy, and even a sense of hope was hard to maintain. I didn't know why I felt so disconnected. Even my old form of therapy, walking in the forest, didn't seem to help. Restless and dissatisfied, I was working at a cigar store in a hotel when a regular customer offered me a job in Vancouver, British Columbia. At first I refused, wary of making the move, but one day I decided to tell him I'd take it.

A few weeks later, I boarded a train for the West Coast. Over the next year I worked in restaurants, bookstores and offices. I lived in Vancouver at first, then moved to the suburbs. I saved enough money to take a few university courses, and this created the first enthusiasm I'd had for any activity in a long time.

On my first day of Biology 102, students gathered in small groups in the big hall, visiting with one another up and down the aisles. Soon the professor took his place before us, opening his lecture with anecdotes about animal behaviour. He talked about "cleaner fish" in the ocean, small fish that cleaned parasites from the skin of larger fish. Then he told us about "cleaner fish mimics," which, instead of eating parasites, bit pieces from the fins of the bigger fish. I leaned forward, shutting out the whisperings of classmates in the seats around me. I was enchanted by what I was hearing. I knew that some professors had work available in their labs, and after the lecture ended I waited my turn to talk to the burly professor as he unhooked himself from his microphone. When he asked about my interest in the field I stumbled over my words, telling him of my childhood interest in spying on animals. He offered to show me around the lab after the next class, and I left the hall with my notes clutched to my chest, my heart pounding.

In the days that followed, my enthusiasm remained constant. It was as if a bright light shone where previously everything had been grey. I was also taking a geography course, and I enjoyed hearing about the titanic forces that had shaped mountain ranges and picturing the drama of rivers carving canyons in the rock.

I decided to see if I could apply for a student loan for full-time studies. On a bulletin board beside the loan office, I saw a notice explaining how a student could get one semester's student loan forgiven by volunteering. I looked through the accompanying list of organizations, and one name stood out: O.W. L.— Orphaned Wild Life. I remembered the great grey owl, Grayl, in Renata's back yard, with his huge rounded head. I could still see his yellow saucer eyes with their perpetually startled look as he tracked Renata across the yard. I'd lost touch with Renata years before, but seeing raptors always reminded me of the time we'd spent together. Now I might have the chance to get close to birds of prey again. I resolved to call O.W. L. as soon as I got home.

3

O. W. L.

A FEW SATURDAYS later, I awoke early, having arranged over the phone to show up at O.W. L. by 9:30. After riding a multitude of buses, I found myself walking down a country road that supposedly led to the wildlife centre. As I walked farther and farther, I began to wonder if I was headed in the right direction. When I saw the sign for O.W. L., I was greatly relieved.

My disorientation returned as I surveyed the centre for the first time. I had pictured a large building with high ceilings, like a warehouse or a barn. Nothing had led me to expect the sprawling one-level house I saw before me. I approached the front door hesitantly. Could this really be a rehabilitation centre for birds? A friendly blonde woman let me in and directed me to the dining room. From a hallway on the right, I could hear scrubbing sounds. A washer and dryer kept up a steady hum and rattle in the background.

When I told the woman at the dining room table that I was a new volunteer, she gestured with her coffee cup towards a young woman walking down the hall. The young woman introduced herself and invited me to accompany her. She pointed out what she called the bird of prey room, but we kept going past it to a smaller room. Here, she explained, birds other than raptors were housed temporarily before being transported to another centre. O.W.L. specialized in birds of prey, but my first job would involve working with these other birds.

The woman gave me a brief description of what to do, directed me to the supplies I'd need, then vanished into the raptor room. I walked into a small area containing a sink. The phone rang many times as I readied the supplies, and I overheard snatches of conversations about getting lumber for a cage, looking after baby robins that had fallen from a nest and arranging a school tour.

In the small room, dog crates of various sizes sat on a large table at waist height. I pulled on a pair of rubber gloves, smoothing them over my wrists as I looked around. Looking back at me through the wire grating of a medium-sized kennel cab was a gull. An adult male glaucous-winged gull, I'd been told. Greenish feces leaked through the kennel cab's grating onto the table. The cage was cleaned every day, the young woman had said, but gulls were apparently very messy. Remembering the smirk on the supervisor's face, I figured this was something of an initiation. I had warm, sudsy water in one small bucket at my feet and rinse water in another. A clean kennel cab lined with newspapers, containing a clean water dish and a full food dish, waited across the room.

I looked again at the gull. He gazed back through small, pale eyes. Gulls used their beaks as weapons, I knew. So maybe I should try a body grab, then hold his beak together with my free hand. Given the height of the cabs, I'd be unable to see once I reached inside unless I bent over double. I felt for the catch on the grating, my fingers groping awkwardly through the extra inch of room in the rubber gloves. The gull made little threatening darts towards my hand with his beak. I fumbled for a moment longer, then heard a click as the catch gave. I let the door open and sit slightly ajar against my sweatshirt.

Suddenly the gull leapt for the opening. The kennel cab bucked as I frantically squashed my stomach against the open cage door. I felt a squelch on my shirt and smelled the acrid stench of feces. The gull flapped against the door for another few seconds, then subsided. Giving the door a firm push shut with my hand, I bent over and peered in. The bird stood at the back of the cage on a mess of churned newspaper cemented with green. His eyes glinted, and his snowy white head was streaked with crusty brown.

"Okay, this is it," I said aloud. I swung the door open and plunged my arms in, feeling for the bird. His beak grabbed at my rubber-coated hands but kept sliding off. This time, instead of drawing back as his head darted forward for a strike, I shoved my hands past and grabbed the firm, thick body. I lowered my head and gingerly stuck my face into the opening to make sure I had a good grip. Then, stepping back, I drew the bird's squirming body towards me, careful to hold it around the meatiest part.

The newspapers came along with him, and the room filled with a smell that made my eyes water. The gull doubled his beak against his breast in an attempt to pry himself free of my hand. I held tight, turning towards the clean cage. With a loose slop, his bowels let go, and feces hit my jeans with a splash. I threw back my head and laughed.

Someone called out, "You all right in there?"

"I'm fine," I called back. I looked down at the gull, held well away from me now. The terror in his eyes stopped my breath. Ashamed of my outburst, I hurriedly set him in the clean cage and pinched the closure firmly, hearing it click. I grabbed a large towel and draped it over the front of his new cab for privacy.

I crossed the room and peered into the old cab. Even the roof was smeared with feces. I put my hand to my hair, then quickly removed it, feeling the sticky matter twined through the strands. I began to attack the cage with vigour. I would ask the volunteer supervisor why the gull was here and when he could go outside, I thought. Things I should have asked before I started with him. On the other side of the wall, in the big room, I could hear the sounds of scrubbing. Maybe soon I'd be working with the birds of prey I knew were housed there. I pictured myself scrubbing and rinsing under the watchful, wary gaze of an eagle. A rush of happiness surged through me.

I SETTLED INTO a new routine of Saturdays at O.W.L. I spent most of my time cleaning cages. More experienced volunteers moved the raptors from dirty cages to clean ones. On the second Saturday, however, I held the legs of a barn owl as he lay on his back while the supervisor's fingers lightly probed him for injuries. His legs were much slimmer and less feathered than those of the snowy owl I had held so long ago for Renata. His eyes too were different, a deep shoe-polish black that reflected tiny replicas of the ceiling's lights back at me. I reached tentatively for a light towel to cover the owl's face and was rewarded with a nod of approval from the supervisor. She traced the alignment of bones in the bird's wings, searching for anything amiss. When I reached towards the wings, she nodded her permission for me to place my fingers where hers had been. I ran them lightly along the thin tapered bones, surprised that such a delicate structure could support the owl's weight in the air. After the bird was placed on the scale and its weight recorded on the waiting case sheet, the supervisor whisked the barn owl from the room. I leaned forward to read its weight. Just over a pound. No wonder the bones could be so light. The bird appeared much heavier than it was.

In the Saturdays that followed, I learned to catch barn owls in my gloved hands. Once, when no one else was available, I decided to move a red-tailed hawk to a clean cage. The power of his legs and feet surprised me. The hawk almost slipped a foot free to claw me, but I managed to hold on precariously as I manoeuvred him to his new cage. Later, when I nervously told the supervisor of my accomplishment, she raised an eyebrow, then smiled.

By the time six months had passed, I'd handled between fifty and a hundred barn owls, in addition to many other species of owls and hawks. I had a knack for catching birds and found myself able to communicate this to new volunteers. Gradually, I took on increasing responsibility for volunteer orientation and supervision.

Injured and orphaned barn owls were in the majority among the raptors the centre housed. But, as I learned, their numbers at O.W.L. painted a deceptive picture of

their numbers in the wild. Unable to survive cold winters, barn owls nested in the mild climate of the West
Coast, with a small pocket of them living in southern
Ontario. The entire Canadian population was estimated
to be only between 300 and 500 birds. Farm landscapes
were prime habitat for the white and sandy-brown bird.

In the raptor room at O.W.L., I always heard the barn
owls before I saw them. Their hissing was amplified by
the cardboard box they often huddled in. One large
indoor cage sometimes held as many as five barn owl
babies. Cardboard boxes placed inside the cages provided
the young birds with shelter, and even the adults scurried
into the boxes when first introduced to them. In the wild,
barn owls sought out farm buildings or natural cavities
like hollowed-out trees to nest in, so the boxes were
miniature versions of those. The other species of owls at
the centre sought more natural cover, such as leafy
branches, in their cages.

As I studied the case sheets for the barn owls one
Saturday morning, the three orphaned owls I was due to
catch next seethed in their box like a small hive of bees.
I looked for the date of admission of each bird and for
information on its injuries and any medicine being
administered. I never knew which birds would be in the
raptor room from one week to the next. It might take
a while to determine which ones were missing from the
weekend before. Sometimes a bird had been moved to

an outside cage to facilitate its recovery. I always hoped
for that. But sometimes the news was sad, and I would
have to deal with the death of a bird I'd held in my
hands the week before.

On mornings after windy nights, the centre always
received calls about birds that had hit windows or vehicles. One of the centre's directors was on call for bird
rescues twenty-four hours a day. She kept a list of volunteers who were willing to rescue or pick up injured birds,
sorted by geographic location. Sometimes the S.P.C.A.
already had the bird contained; sometimes a member of
the public had captured the bird, often a small owl, and
placed it in a box. Sometimes, the rescues involved nets
and chases similar to my snowy owl experience with
Renata.

If the birds O.W. L. volunteers collected were already
dead, their bodies were stored in the freezer until a rep-
resentative from the Fish and Wildlife branch of the
Ministry of Environment could pick them up. The ministry would give the bodies out to people who had ob-
tained permits for taxidermy. One week, riding the bus
to the rehab centre, I saw a dead barn owl tumbling
in the wake of a semi, the bundle of feathers and small
bones finally coming to rest softly at the side of the road.

I put the case sheets for the rescued baby barn owls
back in their slots. The birds couldn't see me yet, because
the opening of their cardboard box faced away from the

cage door, but my footsteps, the rustling of my clothes and my breathing had already alerted them.

It was possible to transfer a whole batch of barn owl babies from one cage to another right in their box, with a heavy towel stretched securely over the front. But though this method was less stressful for the birds, it did not allow us to make a quick individual examination of each baby. By running an index finger and thumb along either side of a bird's breastbone, its keel, you could estimate the bird's weight, always a crucial component in determining how well a bird was progressing.

I donned a pair of light welder's gloves, then checked the clean cage to which I'd be transferring the babies. I made sure there was a fresh bowl of water, newspaper lining the bottom, a laundered sheet over the newspaper and a cardboard box big enough for three. Their daily meal was twelve dead mice, which lay in three piles close to the box opening.

A slant of sunlight warmed my arm through the room's small window. It was windy outside, and I could see billowing trees in the distance. The bushes lining the driveway to O.W.L. flattened and inflated with each new gust. A tingle of anticipation slid along my spine, something I felt each time I reached for a bird of prey. In one smooth motion, I opened the cage door, leaned in and thrust my gloved left hand into the cardboard box. Talons snatched at the glove, then held fast. I slid my hand from the box. One baby barn owl was now latched onto my thumb, and I fastened my right hand around its long legs. The bird, a male, opened his small, pale beak and let loose a raspy scream that shook his entire body. He was fourteen inches tall, and white baby fuzz covered most of his head and body. Both pale-clawed feet gripped my gloved hand with every shred of strength they possessed. As I leaned against the cage door to close it, I felt an intense sting, then a pinch. One of the owl's sharp talons had gone through a seam in my glove. Like a hot needle, I thought. I turned towards the new cage, moving as smoothly as I could. I didn't want to jostle the bird and drive the embedded talon in deeper. The owl's screams continued, falling away briefly as he gulped more air, then rising again. In accompaniment, the other babies kept up a steady steampipe hiss.

Leaning through the open door of the clean cage, I placed the baby owl on his hocks in the box opening, hoping he'd release me and leap inside. He crunched down harder for a second, causing me to wince, then pushed away from my hand and dove into the box. The screaming stopped abruptly, as if a faucet had been turned off. But the air still vibrated around my ears as I turned back to the remaining babies.

The capture and move of the next baby was uneventful, but the third owl refused to be lured from the box by my glove. I turned the open part of the box towards me.

Then, as the owl jumped towards me feet first, I thrust
my gloved hand into his path. He latched on with both
feet. I lifted him as I had the others, with my free hand
wrapped around his upper legs. I could approximate the
ages of the babies by noting each one's transition from
downy to adult feathers. Older than his boxmates by several days, this owl had caramel-coloured feathers peeking
through the baby fuzz on his head and upper body. Just
below his chest, a layer of white down encircled his hips
like a ballerina's tutu. I lifted my hands and stood the
owl in the air before me, his white legs hanging long and
straight below him. He fixed his sooty eyes on mine and
screamed with rage. I recognized the essence and mystery
of a wild, nocturnal barn owl in this bristling baby. His
vitality sent a jolt through me. I placed the baby near
the opening of the cardboard box in the clean cage and
watched him scramble in to join the others, the box rocking with the force of his entry.

Now that the owls did not require my full attention,
I could tune in to the other occupants in the raptor room.
In the next cage I heard a shifting, then a thump, indicating that something large had come to rest. I realized
that the screeching babies might have been grating on
someone else's nerves, too. An adult eagle was housed in
the big cage, hidden behind a sheet.

I had caught my first eagle at O.W.L. after a month
of Saturdays. I was brave and willing, and my supervisor

recognized this in me and fostered it. When catching
owls and hawks, I seemed to have a sixth sense of what
the birds would do next, and my hands would move there
to meet them. Because of this, I began catching eagles
far earlier in my training process than was usual. Not all
volunteers wanted to tangle with eagles, but I was drawn
to these fabulous birds from the beginning.

On one of my shifts at O.W. L., I'd paused in the hallway leading to the bird rooms, watching a volunteer who
was holding a juvenile eagle. I knew she was experienced
at dealing with eagles, and she stood calmly with the
bird. The eagle's head was covered by a towel. Drawing
closer, I noted the huge yellow feet bunched together in
the volunteer's hand. The toes were loosely closed, their
deadly power dormant.

From the room behind me, I could hear the sounds
of scrubbing. I should help with the cleaning, I thought.
But I stayed where I was, cataloguing every detail of
the volunteer's hold on the big bird. The eagle's upper
body lay across the woman's left forearm, and her left
hand anchored the eagle's left wing against its body. Her
right hand held both of the eagle's legs just above the
ankle. Knuckles up, her fingers were threaded between
the eagle's legs; one leg was held between her thumb and
index finger, the other between her index and middle
fingers.

I spoke hesitantly. "Can I carry him back in?"

She looked at me for a second, then motioned me closer with a tilt of her head.

I received the eagle's upper body across my left forearm first, the bird's head still tucked securely from sight under the towel. After I had placed my right hand on the eagle's legs in a replica of the volunteer's hold, a bit higher up, she gradually relinquished the bird to me.

I stood frozen, hugging the eagle awkwardly. The bird had barely stirred during the transfer. My heart thudded in my throat. My left arm trembled, but I concentrated and managed to hold it still, not wanting to provoke any response from the eagle.

I was pleased to find that my hands and arms seemed to know how tightly to hold the eagle, establishing a firm, even pressure. The bird's bunched feet lay inert. His three front toes arched forward, half closed. The long, curved talon of his backward-facing toe rested between the others.

My senses were on full alert. I heard a bucket being set down in the next room and the crinkle and snap of newspapers being opened in preparation for cage lining. From the main part of the house, I could hear a telephone conversation: "Does it have a hooked beak? How high in the tree is it?" The wump of the washer and squeak of the dryer carried down the hall.

After a minute, I noticed that the eagle I held smelled like old blood. Inspecting his feet closely, I could make out tiny pieces of carrion on the underside of one talon.

Another volunteer poked her head in from the closest room and nodded. I stepped forward gingerly, testing my cargo's response. I could feel the eagle's tension, like a guitar string plucked and then held. Carefully I eased my way into the other room, heading towards the large wall cage standing open and clean. A dead white rat lay in the cage near a ceramic bowl of water.

The floor of the cage was just below waist height, and I walked forward until the cage hit my hips. I felt someone lean the door against me, and then a hand reached over and whisked the towel from the eagle's head. Startled dark-chocolate eyes snapped to my face. I swung the bird's legs towards the cage floor, rotating him to a standing position just as he started to struggle. He leapt forward into the cage, then twirled in a circle to face me. I closed the door and latched it, my breath coming fast. Someone clapped me on the back. I'd held my first eagle, and my grin threatened to split my face.

4

CREATURES OF THE WILD

I CONTINUED TO spend my Saturdays
at O.W. L. over the next few years.
During the week I attended university, concentrating
on biology and rounding out my course load with geography. Fascinated by both animal behaviour and the way
rivers carve out canyons, I discovered another interest: the
journals and letters of explorers, with their descriptions of
vast, uncharted wilderness. I read as many of these as
I could get my hands on.

Summers, I worked at the university's behavioural
ecology lab, sitting on a hard stool in a tiny trailer. The
lab specialized in predator/prey interactions. Since the

more glamorous work of assisting with killer whale studies was already spoken for, I had decided to try insects. As part of a study of a wasp that preyed on aphids, the lab was cloning aphids, and my job was to collect the new clones, exact genetic replicas of their parents, and put them into their own vials.

I had to be vigilant about keeping the aphid clones separate from the regular aphids, since there was no way to tell them apart if they got mixed up. I also did "grunt" work at the lab, planting a certain number of plants each week, taking cuttings and collecting a plant called broom from around the university.

One hot afternoon, I sat staring into a small vial that contained the leaf and stem of a plant. I held the vial to the light, straining my eyes. I was looking for the tiny, pale-green dots that signified the presence of baby aphids. A bead of sweat rolled down my temple in the brightly lit room. I imagined myself inside the little jungle world, a miniature person searching for minuscule leaf-coloured creatures.

A persistent sound drew my attention from the search. Strangely enough, it sounded like crickets. Trust me to hear crickets in broad daylight in a stifling trailer, I thought. I tried to concentrate, but the cricket sounds intensified again, and soon I put down my vial, stood up and slid open the door to the narrow hallway. I walked along the hall, then stopped outside the door where the sound seemed loudest. I slid it open and stepped inside to blessed cool darkness. When I closed the door behind me, faint light greyed its edges, allowing me to see. Crickets were loose on the floor, on the shelves, on the counter. Lowering myself gingerly, I sat down, awash in memories of summer nights in Winnipeg. I wanted to stay there, let the seductive creaking flow over my skin. I was no longer sure if I wanted to devote my life to biology. The objectivity that experiments demanded was completely understandable; it was meant to keep the results from being skewed in favour of the researcher's beliefs. But I always wanted to understand how the creatures *felt.* There was a gnawing dissatisfaction in the pit of my stomach that never quite disappeared. It went deeper than school or science or boyfriends (what little I knew of them); it seemed to be a fundamental hole inside of me that nothing could fill.

Sighing, I stood to leave the cricket room. I didn't have permission to be there; my presence could ruin some elaborate experiment. I returned to the cramped room down the hall. For the rest of the afternoon, I amused myself by thinking of the adult aphids as little lime-green muscle cars, souped-up back legs raising their rear ends high in the air.

MORE AND MORE, whether working, riding the bus, studying or relaxing at home with a book, I thought of the wide-open spaces of Delta. It seemed to me that even if I'd been transplanted there directly from the Prairies and set down with my eyes closed, I would have been able to tell the land was flat by the way the wind blew. It was a strong bluster that had travelled a long way, from somewhere out over the ocean, without the diversion of hill or mountain. I wondered often about the new birds that had come in to O.W. L. since I'd been there last.

The centre had moved from the director's house to newly built quarters on the property. Though the move was chaotic, everyone quickly became accustomed to the larger, better-organized space. There was now a much greater variety of cages for recovering birds, and, with a larger medical room, more space for donated medications and bandages. Paperwork and records were filed more systematically in the large office. The foyer and front office became convenient meeting places for the tour groups that frequented the centre in ever greater numbers.

In the new centre, birds labelled non-releasable lived in outside cages. This area, open to the public on certain days, had a walkway winding in front of the bank of cages. A buffer zone of plants and flowers stood between the curious visitors and the chain-link or wire sides of the cages. The majority of the birds were calm around people, and several, like Lucy, the red-tailed hawk, were trained to leave the property with volunteers for educational talks.

Most of the volunteers at O.W. L. were women and girls, and it was through Lucy that I first learned of the connection a woman and a raptor could develop. I'd watch the hawk's patience with a fumbling new volunteer as the woman learned to hold the bird on the glove with the leash wrapped securely through her fingers. I was struck by the kind-heartedness that emanated from Lucy, some-thing I had never expected to find in a bird of prey. As time passed, Lucy taught me much about the individual variation in the personalities of these birds, as well as how to become close to a creature that does not enjoy touch as humans do. Lucy's eyes and her postures gave off affection that I could see only when I shed my human need to touch and interfere. I saw other volunteers strug-gle to nurture injured birds of prey without the solace of touching. Some could not help it but had to stroke and speak soothingly, despite the obvious signs of stress in the patient. I tried to take my cues from the birds themselves, watching closely how they behaved with one another.

The eagles at O.W. L. continued to draw my attention above all other birds. Early in my days there, I'd been introduced to eagle catching in an outdoor cage. Now I did it more often, but I still remembered how nervous and excited I had been the first time.

The volunteer supervisor had asked me to help her move Chatty Kathy, a large juvenile eagle renowned for the continuous sounds she emitted. We could often hear her chortling from a distance, and when people appeared the noise increased in frequency. As I waited outside the eagle's cage for the supervisor to join me, I heard a deep croaking. I stepped closer, peering through the tiny wire-and-slat-covered window. Immediately, the bird spotted me.

The eagle stretched her neck to its full extent and swayed back and forth several times, her beak held high, her eyes fixed on my face. A displeased-sounding croak came from the black beak, ending in a high-pitched whine. Kathy was probably in her third year. Her beak remained dark, but her brown head and neck were spattered with white. The mixture gave her an unkempt appearance.

I drew in a shaky breath. We were going to weigh Chatty Kathy and then move her to a larger cage. I didn't know if it was true or not, but it seemed to me that juvenile raptors were a less predictable lot than their adult counterparts. They were more apt to develop dependencies on humans than were the wary adults. Even in the short time I'd been at O.W.L., I'd learned that a socialized eagle was not necessarily more friendly, just less fearful.

The volunteer supervisor approached in a business-like fashion, carrying two sets of heavy gloves and several large blankets. At her instruction, I donned a pair of the gloves. She laughed at my expression. "You're only my back-up," she said, "but you never know what can happen!" Her comment did nothing to calm my beating heart. I took one last look in through the window. Kathy's eyes locked on mine, and I felt her razor-sharp readiness getting under my skin. Stress was pouring off her in waves, and I realized, with shame, that by staring in at her I had compounded it.

The supervisor explained that I was to herd the eagle towards her waiting hands. I stared at her, incredulous. *Herd the eagle?* She explained further that I should hold the blanket in front of me to make myself look more imposing.

Before I had time to digest all this, the supervisor dragged the door open and gave me a gentle push inside. The air was instantly filled with a roaring of feathers and movement. Terrified, I lifted my blanket against the onslaught and stumbled forward, unsure of my footing. Just as suddenly, the cage became quiet. As I lowered the blanket, I saw that the supervisor had the huge brown eagle pinioned neatly in her arms. She held the juvenile bird as one would a baby, except that the bird was angled more vertically. "Good job," she said as she prepared to turn towards the door. I nodded in a daze, unsure how I'd pulled it off. The juvenile eagle was almost inert, and some part of me was sad to see her so subdued. Her eyes were far from dead, however; they crackled with energy and spirit. I tore my eyes away and slipped ahead of the supervisor, anxious to see Chatty Kathy in her new, larger cage. I knew this was a stage on the way to her release.

The eyes of another eagle I had dealt with at O.W. L.

continued to haunt me. The paralyzed female adult lay
on her back on a cold steel table in the middle of the busy
back room of a veterinary clinic. A woman walking her
dog near a ravine had found the helpless eagle and
brought her to the clinic. They had phoned O.W. L. to
come for her. As I made my way towards the eagle, vet
technicians rushed by with dogs. Someone examined
a large dog on a table only ten feet away. The eagle's eyes
stopped my breath. Her mute anguish seeped into my
bones.

I lifted the bird's still body. There was no movement of any body part. Yet I could feel a resistance that
reminded me of environmental protesters I had seen on
television, going limp as they were hauled clear of
logging trucks. The resistance in the eagle's eyes was
spellbinding.

I carried the bird to a side room, where I turned out
the lights after placing a towel on the table for her to lie
on. A flighted creature forced to be still must endure the
cruellest of punishments, I thought. I propped the eagle
on her side with another towel so that she faced the wall
and then left her alone. I felt sure she would prefer it.

X-rays confirmed that the eagle had a spinal injury.
She was euthanized by one of the vets, and I held her
until the life ebbed from her magnificent eyes.

Birds that recovered from their injuries at O.W. L.
were released to the wild. Barn owls were placed in barns

whose owners had erected nesting boxes high on the inside or the outside of the building, using specifications given to them by the centre. With the exception of juveniles, most other raptors were released at the site where they had been found. Many birds of prey are monogamous, and the rehabilitated bird's mate might be waiting. Since juveniles would leave their nest territory anyway, new areas, rich in food for that species, would be chosen for the young birds. Because of their social nature and the huge distances they can fly, bald eagles were released either on the O.W. L. property or at the end of the road, where the dyke wound along the Boundary Bay shoreline. One afternoon I was thrilled to witness the release of an eagle we called Terra Nova.

I had had a memorable encounter with Terra early in my volunteer days at O.W. L. The chocolate-brown juvenile had been found abandoned by her parents in an area by the ocean not far from the centre. Staff at O.W. L. speculated that, given the behaviour of this youngster, the juveniles from her nest had become accustomed to people. I knew that could be a problem for wild juveniles, leading them to approach people too closely. Socialized raptors, because of a lack of fear, could also harbour aggression towards humans.

The young eagle's big feet were bright yellow, contrasting sharply with the dark brown of her plumage. First-year juveniles usually showed few telltale traces of the white head and tail that would gradually appear over the next five years. Terra's size made the slatted wood cage, approximately twenty feet long and eight feet wide, seem small. The wooden cages, slated for replacement with larger wood and wire ones as soon as enough money had been raised, allowed staff and volunteers to observe the birds when they were first moved outside.

Restless and fiery, Terra stalked back and forth along the heavy spruce bough that held her, occasionally tearing at the branch with her feet. Bark littered the grass beneath her perch, and I could see that in no time the branch would be bare. As I peered through the tiny wire window at the bird, I shuffled my feet on the ground. Terra's head whipped around, her dark eyes focussing on my face. Without hesitation she opened her wings and flew for the door. Shocked, I jumped back from the window. I saw a giant brown shape looming just before I ducked instinctively. The wood of the flimsy door groaned as she hit it. The padlock rattled in the hasp. A hard rap of bone on wood and a whoosh of wings were followed by silence. The air settled, and I knew the eagle was gone. Carefully, I looked through the window. Terra stood stretched tall on the bough, her head small at the end of her arched neck, her eyes glinting. I prepared to duck as she looked at me again, but this time she turned away and gazed out over the field instead. "Wow." I spoke aloud, charged by the encounter.

I thought of all this the afternoon I watched Terra Nova explode from the hands of O.W.L.'s director into the sky. The eagle flew high above the mud flats, ignoring the small crowd of spectators gathered to witness her release. I shaded my eyes, holding back my hair in the strong wind. In the distance, I could see a lone eagle perching on deadfall down by the dyke. Terra flew in that direction, spooking the perching eagle. She disappeared into the distance, flying hard behind the other bird. Someone made a wry comment about not being unhappy to see *that* one go. Many of the group bore scars from the formidable young eagle.

Although I knew that not all of the birds at O.W.L. were suitable for release, I resisted the idea of a non-releasable label being placed on any of them. Broken legs that didn't fully heal, soft tissue and bone injuries in wings, head trauma: these were some of the reasons the birds had to be kept in captivity. A barely discernible droop in one wing might become obvious when the bird was placed in a larger flight cage. I knew the logic of the label, but I struggled with it as I watched a short-eared owl pouncing happily on a mouse, her infirmity not immediately apparent. I worried about when the barred owl with severe head trauma would finally be tagged non-releasable, despite knowing that the alternative was euthanasia.

At night, I would sometimes dream about the birds.

In a watery dreamworld I would move across the field towards their cages, reaching for latches, pulling doors open all over the property. Amidst the flutter of wings, I would turn to watch the sky as the air filled with the shriek of pinions and the hum of wind against straining bone and sinew. Once the noise abated, I would turn slowly to see the injured birds hobbling across the field, wings half outstretched, eyes locked on those flying away. I began running through the field, trying to catch them. From these dreams I would wake up crying.

I always felt as excited as a new volunteer when I was involved in a release. By now, I had become a volunteer supervisor at O.W.L., and I had scraped together enough money to get a car on the road. That allowed me to participate in releases done away from the centre.

One Saturday afternoon, I found myself driving along a country road with a young great horned owl sheltered in a kennel cab in the back seat. We were headed to a release site in Campbell Valley Park, close to the U.S. border. It was a good habitat for great horned owls, rich in rodents and rabbits and close to farmland areas should the bird decide to leave the park. A wide wood-chip trail and a ravine bordered the park's thick woods. A river ran through the park, and small meadows were interspersed throughout the forest.

As I pulled to the side of the road, I remembered the crowds of people walking around the park's giant barn and heritage buildings and visiting booths at the environmental fair held last summer on the site. Now the field was deserted, and the caretaker already had his porch light on for the coming night. Horseback riding was common here, though I saw no riders today.

I unloaded the kennel cab from the car and set off with it down a gravel access road, awkwardly shortening each right step as the crate bounced against my leg. The towel draped over the front grate lifted slightly in the breeze but stayed anchored under the kennel cab's handle and my fingers. The owl clacked his beak with each bump.

On the grass just past the blackened doorway of the old barn, I paused to admire the late-afternoon light that softened the edges of the dusty-grey building. This was my ritual. Whenever I took part in a release, I always made sure to look around first at the world I'd be sending the bird back into. I turned the owl's crate to face away from the sun. My long shadow shifted, black whip arms stretching like licorice before me. After a minute, I reached down and carefully popped the catch on the door. I moved to stand behind the crate, swinging the door open and lifting the towel at the same time.

At first there was no movement inside, only a kind of shocked stillness. Then the crate rocked back against my legs, and the owl catapulted from confinement. Huge heather wings folded and rose before my face, but no more than a faint hush, hush reached my ears. Light gilded the bird's wings, warming them almost to cinnamon. The owl's hanging legs lifted up and tucked straight back, dispelling any notion that he was of this earthbound world where I stood. He turned his head once in that eerie, seamless way owls have, and I caught a glimpse of his huge sulphur-coloured eyes before he swung around and flew straight towards the sun and the forest, his shadow tagging black over the grass.

I wished I could stay and eavesdrop on the owl's first night back in the woods, listen to the deep hoots that would electrify the other great horned owls in the vicinity. I knew the resident pairs might oust him. It depended on the size of the owl population and the available territory. But given the adaptability of great horns and the number of small forests in the area, I thought he'd do fine. I wished him well and walked through the dying light back to my car.

5

A GATHERING OF EAGLES

E VERY WINTER there is a large
conglomeration of bald eagles at
Squamish, British Columbia, about a two-hour drive
from Vancouver. December and January are the peak
months for the salmon run in the Squamish and
Cheakamus Rivers, and thousands of eagles from all
along the West Coast gather to partake in the feast. I'd
always longed to see this event for myself, and several
years into my time at O.W.L. I finally managed to arrange
it. I made plans with an O.W.L. volunteer named Mark
to participate in the annual eagle count at Brackendale,
on the outskirts of Squamish.

It was overcast with high clouds the day of the count. Mark and I set out from North Vancouver along the famous Sea to Sky Highway. The highway's name is apt. The road winds high above Howe Sound, a deep-cut fjord with mountainous islands rising from the icy blue water.

A little embarrassed by my avidity, I looked constantly past my friend in the driver's seat to the distant layers upon layers of blue folded mountains. A crooked branch jutting out at right angles to the water seemed the perfect size for an eagle perch. I knew that any eagles we saw as we drove would be travellers on their way to the bounty of salmon. I scanned the trees and the sky in search of them.

By now, I had been exposed to many eagles: eagles recuperating from wounds, pesticide poisoning and broken bones; eagles in various stages of recovery trying out their wings in large cages as volunteers watched closely for any signs of weakness. I had followed the birds of prey as they burst from the hands of volunteers and had had the heady honour of releasing a few myself. I always watched greedily as they powered away. The prospect of seeing so many of the birds together in their natural habitat today had me on the edge of my seat.

Our car clung tight to the snow-dusted mountain flanks, nose to tail with a surprising amount of traffic. Many of these cars would be on their way to Whistler, the world-class ski resort that lay beyond Squamish along this route. The numerous rockfall warning signs we passed as we drove were a reminder of the danger that is also part of the Sea to Sky Highway's mystique.

As we approached Squamish, I spotted a large juvenile bald eagle in a tree beside the road. From her size, I guessed that she was a female. As we watched, she released her grip on the branch where she perched and bounced to the sky. The spread of her primary feathers reminded me of a piano player's fingers across a keyboard. The bird's long legs dropped underneath her at first, her yellow feet clenched like fists, then tucked up behind her. In an instant, she was out of sight, leaving behind only a rebounding branch and a shower of icicles.

We knew the eagle was a juvenile from her colouring. Research findings vary about the precise timing of the stages, but it is observable that juveniles moult towards their adult colouring, gradually gaining a greater proportion of white feathers on their heads and tails, with their eyes lightening to yellow from brown and their beaks from smoky black to yellow. At sometime around four years old, a juvenile's head is mainly white, with some brown streaking; its tail is in the same condition. From a distance, a juvenile this age may appear to be an adult, but further whitening will take place over the next two years. By the age of six, an eagle is as white as it's going to become, with some birds retaining faint brown or grey streaks in their head feathers.

Studies have shown that although juvenile and adult bald eagles have similar skeletal dimensions, the young-sters have longer tail and wing feathers, which makes them appear larger than adults. It is believed these longer feathers help the young birds obtain lift in updrafts. Immature birds tend to fly more slowly than adults and are more wind-dependent. Adults, with their shorter feathers, have better capabilities for fast, directed flight and a better capacity to fly quickly upwind, as when they fly up to land on their nests. Because juveniles are not nesting, this is less important for them.

I knew from the reading I'd done that eagles tend to soar or glide whenever possible, since this requires much less energy than that needed to flap their large wings continuously. Eagles tend to have three patterns of flight: ascending a thermal, then gliding down for several miles before finding another one; circling steadily downwind in a series of rising air masses; or using a natural updraft created by a cliff or other rise in the land. The birds can travel at speeds of fifty miles an hour or more, covering vast distances.

The image of the juvenile flying was still with me as we pulled into the parking lot of the Brackendale Art Gallery, headquarters of the eagle count. Inside the rustic building, groups of warmly clad people stood about talk-ing and drinking from mugs of coffee or hot chocolate. A large chart on the wall blocked out the areas for the count; numbers would fill the blank spaces under each column by the end of the day. The town of Squamish and the lower Cheakamus River needed counters, so Mark and I volunteered our services to the guide for that section, a man named Tom. "Sparse pickings in those areas," he told us. "I'll need people with sharp eyes." Mark and I exchanged a smile. No problem there.

The three of us piled into Tom's truck and set off in search of eagles. While the men chatted, I peered out at the snow-covered landscape. Once we had passed the houses around the gallery, the river came into view. Craning upright, I caught a glimpse of a tree on the other side of the water that seemed to have more eagles than branches.

"Look!" I managed to choke out.

"Not our area for counting," Tom said, but he slowed the truck just the same. Looking more closely, I realized there were even more eagles in the tree than I had thought initially. The white-headed adults were readily visible against the leafless branches; the juveniles, with their brown colouring, were less conspicuous. Tom pulled away after a few minutes, but I pivoted in my seat to keep the "eagle tree" in sight a little longer.

Bald eagles are nomadic, and I knew from my reading that eagle density in particular territories varies according to the abundance of food. The availability of food also affects nesting practices. If the food source is rich, then nests are built closer together. In crowded areas, juveniles unrelated to a nesting pair can sometimes be found perching in the same tree as that pair's nest. In less rich areas, a nesting pair might hold a territory of up to a mile. Researchers in some study areas have observed bald eagles chasing intruding eagles out of a ten-mile radius, but this behaviour is rare; more often, researchers believe, eagles protect their territory by perching visibly high in trees or by emitting a loud territorial call. During salmon runs, eagles from all up and down the coast come together to feed, and squabbles over food and perches are commonplace.

As we drove, I watched the sky for soaring eagles. I knew that large soaring groups are often the signal to other eagles of a bountiful area. Some researchers speculate that eagles can see such groups from as many as fourteen miles away. Research also indicates that eagles are more likely to fish in an area where other eagles are already present.

In addition to being consummate fishers, bald eagles are superlative hunters of other prey. There are well-documented accounts of eagles catching waterfowl, seabirds such as cormorants, and larger birds like whistling swans and snow geese. In the Interior territories, bald eagles are known to prey on waterfowl that have been crippled by hunters; some eagles even time their migration with the winter freeze-up so that the injured birds, swimming in smaller and smaller openings in the ice, are an easy kill. Bald eagles on the San Juan Islands in western Washington state also hunt an introduced species, the European hare. Thinking about this, I was struck again by the bald eagle's adaptability and efficiency.

Tom and Mark and I began looking in earnest for eagles once we reached our specified area. The snow was deep, and at first we watched our footing as much as we did the sky and the trees. We walked towards the sound of the river.

Standing on a spit of snow, I watched the bubbling current. Mark, who'd bragged earlier about his hiking boots being waterproof, parked himself in a small eddy. He looked slim and athletic in the latest in outdoor clothes. By contrast, my clothes were a mixed bag. I was still stuck in the Prairie mentality that says layers, and many of them, are best for cold. I'd shed two layers already, reducing my resemblance to a fat bear. Looking up, I caught a glimpse of a soaring eagle in the distance. "One," I called, pointing out the bird to the others.

We hiked back to the truck and set out for a stream a mile or two away that had slower water and was located approximately under the soaring eagle. As we drew closer, tiny specks in the air took shape as a column of spiralling eagles. "Fifteen," I crowed as the three of us scrambled from the truck. We revised the figure to eighteen as our eyes adjusted to the glare of the grey-white sky.

We pushed through thick undergrowth to get to
the stream, slowing our pace once we saw water glinting
through the bushes. We didn't want to spook the perching eagles we felt sure were there. Stepping into the clear,
we spotted two adult birds in a stand of trees across the
water, their white heads like beacons against the dark
branches. They perched about fifteen feet from each
other and seemed settled and calm. One eagle occasionally inclined its head and peered at the water, but if these
birds were fishing, they were certainly relaxed about it.
After a minute, I noticed that the smaller of the two had
a small bulge just below its throat. "Crop," I said quietly
to Mark, indicating the internal sac that holds food
before it is digested down into the stomach. This bird
had either eaten a small amount recently or held the
remains of a large feed ingested hours before. I'd seen
eagles with a crop as large as a small football. At O.W.L.,
an eagle who'd had surgery to remove the food we
suspected was poisoning him had had a full-sized gull
in his crop.

We looked carefully at the rest of the trees across
the stream but saw no eagles. Then, as we backed away
from the shore, I glanced up at a large tree on our side of
the river and locked eyes with a juvenile eagle about fifty
feet away. My throat worked for a moment as I suppressed
the desire to alert my fellow counters. I didn't want to
break eye contact with the bird. In my peripheral vision,

66

I saw Mark's dark-blue jacket disappear into the brush. I stayed where I was, hungrily taking in the eagle before me. From her size, I thought that the tall juvenile was a female. Her dark eyes seemed friendly, although I knew that was my human imposition of the "warm brown eyes" stereotype. The bird turned her head sideways, contemplating me. Her lack of fear surprised me. Her head was mostly chocolate brown, but her chest was liberally streaked with white, in vertical bars. When she turned back to look across the river, perhaps at the adults, I could see the white feathers that circled her neck and throat like a cowl. As I shifted my attention to her large yellow feet, with their thick, black, curved talons, I heard Mark's voice in the distance. Reluctantly, I moved away.

The river flowed faster in the rest of our counting territory. We saw a few more eagles flying with purpose to what we supposed were fishing areas in the distance. One tree along our route held several juveniles, and Mark and I speculated on their ages by assessing the amount of white on their bodies, although we knew it was impossible to be certain.

After going back to the gallery with Tom to hand in our counting results, Mark and I drove to an area where high eagle volume had been reported. We were rapt as we watched various dramas play out before us. In one tree, two eagles squabbled over a favoured perch. A hundred feet away, behind a log, a raven hurriedly swallowed a strip of fish. Near a bend in the river, a large tree was festooned with eagles. In awe, I counted twenty.

A gracefully gliding immature eagle, probably a male, drew his wings in tight all of a sudden and twirled abruptly to the ground. The speed of his landing was not lost on a big juvenile female nearby, and the young bird flew across the river to see what had drawn the first bird's attention. The soft chuckling of the river was pierced by high-pitched cries as the two eagles squabbled over some food invisible to our eyes. With increasing aggression, the bigger juvenile lifted her chest, reared her head back and half opened her wings, advancing on the smaller bird. He let loose a defensive cry and jumped sideways, clutching his prize. As the female opened her wings further, the male took to the air, a thin scrap of fish clutched in his foot. The female leapt with him and, in a breathtaking manoeuvre, turned herself upside down and wrenched the scrap from his foot. She righted herself with a triumphant croak—and then dropped the piece of fish. A crow darted in and swallowed it. We laughed at the befuddled eagle as she looked at her empty foot, then swung her head around aggressively to look for the culprit. The crow was perching on a stump not far away, wiping his beak against the wood.

In a distant tree, I could see a giant mass of sticks that looked like a nest. January is nesting season for coastal bald eagles, and adults begin in December to prepare the nests used in previous years, adding branches as needed and repairing damage wrought by wind and storms. Though a nesting pair tend to use the same nest from year to year, they may also visit and maintain alternative nests in the area.

Coastal eagles lay eggs from late February to early March, northern Interior birds in mid-April. Eggs are incubated for about thirty-five days in a feather-and-greenery–lined nest cup in the middle of the much larger nest. Once hatched, juveniles stay in the nest for ten to thirteen weeks.

Nests range from six to nine feet in diameter, so the number of sticks and branches used in building them is immense. A record nest in northern California measured ten feet across and twenty feet deep and weighed six thousand pounds. Given that juvenile eagles reach full stature at between eight and ten weeks, it is easy to see that a smaller nest would be too crowded for two babies with six-foot wingspans plus their adult mother.

To accommodate such weights, the trees chosen for nests are usually large old-growth trees with thick, irregular-shaped branches in the upper crown. These form a crotch, or forked base of support, for the nest structure. Over time, nests may begin to list, especially in trees that lack adequate support. Crowns of trees have been known to give way under the weight of an eagle's nest. In coastal habitat, the common nest tree species are Douglas fir, western red cedar, spruce and hemlock. Along rivers, cottonwoods are also used. Rarely are eagles found nesting more than a mile from water, whether river, lake or ocean.

Bald eagles avoid building their nests right at the top of the tree, preferring a thin screen of branches above as protection from inclement weather. Most nests have roost perches close by where the male can sit while the female is on the nest. He assumes a protective posture, often escorting other eagles out of the air space above the nest.

Prevailing wind direction also plays a role in the placement of the nest and the selection of perches. Flying into the wind aids eagles in landing; strong tailwinds make for uncontrolled, haphazard touchdowns. To allow their giant wings through unscathed, there must also be openings in the foliage surrounding the nest. Often there are air corridors leading directly from a local food source to the nest.

It was getting late in the day, and Mark and I needed to head for home. Once we reached the highway, we reflected on how privileged we were, through our work at O.W.L., to know eagles as few people did. We'd heard the rattle their lungs made when pneumonia took hold, the rasping sounds their wings made against wood and cloth. Their blood had splashed on our hands, and during surgeries we'd seen their bones exposed. But nothing compared to seeing them whole and soaring, to hearing their shrieks and warbles in the wild.

6

SETTLING IN

IN THE WEEK after I first met Ichabod,
I thought about her often. I always
responded at a deep level to a new eagle arriving at
O.W.L., but somehow this young bird seemed to exert an
even stronger pull. I could hardly wait to see her again.

As the Saturday volunteer supervisor, though, I had
other duties to attend to before I could check on Ichabod.
One of those was to make sure the daily feeding of the
residents got smoothly underway. Watching a woman
walk by casually swinging a dead rat by its tail, I thought
of the jokes and camaraderie I'd gotten used to at O.W.L.
over the past few years.

Every day, frozen rats, mice and quail were defrosted for the next day's meals for the birds. In addition to rodents and quail purchased from breeders, there were buckets of freshly trapped muskrats, much loved by the eagles, that were left at the door of the care centre each week by a taciturn local trapper. Whenever the centre got fish from the local fishing community, that was fed to the eagles as well.

The rats came curled in frozen balls, with up to five of them intertwined. They had to be pulled apart to let them thaw, which entailed shoving a knife between the bodies and then hammering on the handle. Once forced apart, the frozen rats were contorted in strange positions. Sometimes volunteers would stand them up together, pretending the rats were dancing to various songs. Englebert Humperdinck was a favourite, and strains of "Please re-lease me, let me go, 'cause I don't love you any more-ore" often drifted down the halls. One day, two young volunteers set up a pair of rats so that their paws touched and waltzed them around the table. Another girl grabbed a rat with its head thrown back and swayed it to a raunchy rendition of "Twist and Shout."

In addition to getting the feeding organized, I made sure enough volunteers were assigned to the public tours. Then I checked the case sheets to see which birds were in need of medication and arranged for that to be administered. It was only once all these things were in place that I was free to head for the interim case room—and Ichabod.

Quietly, I lifted the edge of the sheet covering the eagle's cage and looked inside. The floor of the cage was carpeted in Astroturf, which was in turn covered with a thick cotton sheet. Three low stumps were spaced evenly over the surface. Another stump, sawed in half, lay on its side, rough surface up. A set of V notches in the pale-green wall held a branch thicker than my wrist. Eagle feces decorated the sheet in long white streaks. Perches and stumps were always kept away from the walls of the cage, since eagles can project their feces two or three feet backwards.

In amongst the stumps and perches stood Ichabod. Her big yellow feet with their curved black talons looked incongruous against the soft white cotton. Replete from an earlier feeding, she stood flat on one foot. Her other foot, closed like a fist, rested on the sheet ahead of her. I wondered why she had chosen the floor to stand on.

The young eagle looked at me with a mild expression. The contrast between her behaviour and that of the other patients in the room was marked. If I even twitched the sheets of the other cages, I'd hear birds scrambling to escape or to put themselves in the most defensive position. As I opened the door to her cage, the eagle shifted to face me. Her wings opened slowly. She stood with them held awkwardly away from her body, looking like a teenager who wasn't sure what to do with herself. She pulled her wings slowly forward until they cloaked her body, then unfurled them just as slowly, as if doing a strange parody of flying. Twice more she did her slow-motion wing calisthenics.

I'd never observed an eagle at this stage of development. Ichabod was full of latent power and presence, yet the gawky, insecure baby in her was still present. I felt excitement shoot along the back of my neck, but also a familiar apprehension. Would this eagle be releasable in the end? Closing her wings, no longer concerned with me, Ichabod hopped onto the stump in the corner and proceeded to worry a small piece of gristle left over from a previous meal.

"SHAKING IT ROUGH" is prison lingo for a prisoner having a hard time coping with confinement. Injured raptors new to the wildlife centre often exhibited their version of this by refusing to eat. The food at O.W.L. was unfamiliar, and many birds were too sick or injured or stressed by being forced into close quarters with people to bother with food. Sometimes a bird would be so skinny when it came to O.W.L. that a day or two without food would have resulted in death. Force-feeding was one option, but that created even greater stress for the patient, and the combination of stress and injury could kill a bird. In some instances, all that was needed to remedy the situation was a move to an outside cage.

Ichabod ate well, luckily, and she seemed to be settling in nicely. By the time of my next shift at O.W. L., she had been moved to a large corner indoor/outdoor cage. Getting to her cage now meant walking through an unheated roofed area around the back of the care centre. There were six cages in this area. Two were completely under cover, but the other four had both covered and outdoor portions.

The covered area of Ichabod's new cage was fourteen by eighteen feet in size. The cage was bordered on two sides by walls shared with other cages. The two remaining sides of her cage led to the outside area. Half walls were built along these two sides so that she could perch there or fly over. She could also get into the outside part of her cage through a swinging door set in one of the half walls. At first she preferred to fly both ways, but over time she would begin to jump on the swinging door and "ride" it inside with the momentum of her leap.

The outdoor area of Ichabod's cage, thirty-eight feet on its longest side, contained a child's wading pool with logs rolled alongside to allow the eagle easy perching before and after her baths. Each corner of the outdoor section had large horizontal branch perches, and one corner had a raised platform with a stump on top. Chain-link covered the perimeter of the entire cage.

I looked through the small barred window set in the door to Ichabod's cage. Today she was standing on an outside perch with her wings dropped away from her sides, exposing herself to the sun. A volunteer chose that moment to walk on the path between the cages, past the perching eagle. Ichabod turned her head and tracked the woman. I watched the crest of feathers on the back of her head rise until she appeared to be wearing a headdress. The woman was almost by when Ichabod leapt sideways along the branch towards the volunteer, her head low. She kept her eyes pinned on the receding figure.

With a satisfied air, the eagle raised her head and flicked her tail from side to side. Her feathers flattened to sleekness. I knew from my observations of other eagles that what I had watched was an aggressive, territorial move. I shifted my position at the door, and the sound drew her attention. Her gaze sharpened as her eyes fastened on my face. The eagle's crest lifted again, and this time she raised the feathers on her chest and shoulders as well, making herself look larger and even more imposing.

Ichabod opened her wings and lifted off the perch, heading in my direction. She seemed to be intending the flat top of the half wall as her destination. But though she flapped hard, she misjudged the distance, and she dropped from sight behind the wall.

I waited. And waited.

Finally Ichabod appeared, walking through the door in the half wall. She looked so funny that I laughed out loud. She jumped onto a log on the floor six feet from me. Her crest rose again as she stared at the window.

I turned away, setting off to get the food my presence no doubt seemed to promise.

NOBEL PRIZE–WINNING biologist Konrad Lorenz is a familiar name to those who have heard of his imprinted ducks. Imprinting is a complex subject that involves the attachment of a young bird to whatever it perceives as its parent. For species like ducks, which are precocial birds—birds that don't stay in the nest after hatching— imprinting takes place during a particular window of time, usually thought to be between thirteen and sixteen hours after birth. Early imprinting is necessary for such species, since it allows a family of babies to stay together for protection when they leave the nest.

Young raptors are altricial, meaning they stay in the nest while developing, so their imprinting takes place over weeks and months rather than hours or days. According to Nick Fox, in his book *Understanding Birds of Prey,* young raptors have "susceptible sensitive periods." There is imprinting both to the parents, or food source, and to other siblings in the nest. With this imprinting comes the recognition of what to fear.

Human intervention in a young raptor's life derails "normal" imprinting and draws the bird towards people. Because imprinting in bald eagles has not been studied extensively, however, it's difficult to specify the susceptible periods for imprinting eagles to humans. To compound the issue, it is possible for a bird to be partially imprinted or to show a combination of wild and human-imprint traits.

Ichabod reached human hands at approximately eight weeks of age. The sheet sent to O.W. L. from the Kamloops Wildlife Park indicated that the eagle had been hand-fed twice a day from the time of her arrival there on June 20 until July 14. In the wild, though an eight-week-old eaglet would have had food supplied by the parent bird, the food would have been dropped at the eaglet's feet for the eaglet to tear instead of being rendered into pieces, as parents do for younger birds. Today, wildlife centres use eagle-head puppets to drop the food for young birds in cases like this. They use two-way mirrors to avoid being seen, or they put a young displaced eagle with eagle foster parents. The key to a bird's ability to qualify for release back to the wild is that it not associate people with food. For Ichabod, this early hand-feeding, coupled with the stress of captivity, had been enough to foster a dependency. By the time she reached O.W. L. at twelve weeks old, she viewed people as her food source and, as a result, lacked a fear response to the tall creatures who looked nothing like her original parents.

This lack of fear went hand in hand with seeing humans as competitors for food, I soon learned. A number of falconers used the flat lands around O.W. L. as a place to work with their birds, particularly the network

of old roads that led to the abandoned portion of the
airport. Falcons lost by falconers often turned up at the
centre, too. Since some of the birds were leg-banded, we
were able to call their owners to come to pick them up.
One of these falconers, told about Ichabod by a volunteer, came to have a look at her during my shift.

"Is she an imprint?" he asked me.

I didn't know how to answer. I realized that no one
had really addressed the point until now. "Well, she's
socialized to people," I said. "I'm not sure, really."

As we talked, the falconer told me that falcons and
hawks imprinted to people react to a human presence
with defensiveness or aggression, especially if food is
being offered. Many falconers have tales of being attacked
by these socialized birds, he said, stories of talons through
thumbs and scars left on arms. According to him, because
the birds lack a fear response to people, they react to
humans as competitors for food and territory. As I
thought about it, that certainly seemed true of Ichabod.

TO STAND SCANT FEET away from an eagle is exhila-
rating. It is even more so when the eagle approaches you
voluntarily. In all of my years of watching and interacting
with injured eagles at O.W.L., Ichabod was the first bird
to come forward to meet me halfway. My encounters with
eagles to that point had been aimed at alleviating, as best
I could, the fear that pervaded their captive lives. Even

the non-releasable eagles on display to the public moved away when you reached some invisible threshold or boundary of safety. The birds would shift along their perches or fly short spans to maintain their individual distances of comfort. Their behaviour had a ritualized air to it. The birds responded to humans as if we were a tide or some other force of nature.

With these non-releasable birds, savvy volunteers learned, as I had, to respect the "body territory" of each bird. When filling pools, placing food in cages or removing old scraps of food, you would approach the bird at an indirect angle, often turning your body slightly sideways as well to avoid presenting a full frontal threat. Once you'd learned how to do this, you could weave through a cage while the bird stayed still, unspooked, on its original perch. You might need to press against the bubble of space around a bird at times, but you did so with a quiet probing that could only be read as non-threatening.

The safe territories around new patients were much larger, and they tended to fluctuate wildly. When I was getting to know a bird, I would stand outside its cage and try to feel the atmosphere inside with all my senses. Sometimes, for a few breaths, I could sense the charged ambiance of a bird on the edge of panic. In those instances, I would prepare myself to do the bare minimum, sacrificing perfect cage cleaning for the mental health of the bird. I would enter the cage with my joints bent,

crouching low, eyes averted from the occupant. I might
enter sideways, or even backwards, then crab-walk slowly
towards a scrap of food left over from a previous meal.
I'd reach out slowly, eyes down, sneaking my rubber-
gloved fingers over the Astroturf towards the twisted skin
of a rat or the entrails of a rabbit stuck to the green pile.
I'd force myself to breathe slowly, rather than holding
my breath and filling the air with expectation. But sometimes, despite my best efforts, the bird would erupt in a
flurry of flapping and hit the wall or the slatted sides
of the cage.

Once as I retreated from an eagle's cage, pleased to
feel I had not spooked the bird, I was shocked to receive
a punch on the back of the neck from the eagle's closed
foot. Squashed to the ground by the blow, I lay frozen,
wincing inside as the wings crashed around me for
another second. Then, in the blessed quiet of the after-
math, I crept quickly from the cage, unable to slow the
jerky movements of my limbs as I felt the ancient fear
of the hunted shivering through me. Once I stood safely
outside the cage, I thought of how fear and aggression
are linked. Had the eagle attacked me to drive me from
the cage? To "save face"? It hadn't been a full attack,
since the foot that had whacked me was closed. In that
moment, I understood clearly the bird's fear. It had hit
me with a closed foot because grabbing me would have
required engaging in a fight. Eagles of this temperament,

81

SETTLING IN

their nerves vibrating visibly, had huge body territories.
I always hoped that these birds could be moved to the
largest flight cages possible, monitored from a distance
and released shortly afterwards.

Being constantly feared was mentally tiring. I understood why some volunteers wished the birds would get
accustomed to them; it was the human social need to
comfort. But I knew this socialization could cause death
for birds in the wild, as they allowed less well-meaning
people to approach. I believed strongly in socializing
releasable birds as little as possible. That meant no excess
talking, no hanging around to watch the bird when it
knew of your presence, and taking special care around
young and impressionable birds.

I remember once laughing at a joke told to me by
another volunteer, then walking through the swinging
doors to the cage room still chuckling aloud. I sucked
back my laugh as two nervous eagles took to the air
behind their curtained windows, hitting their walls
over and over with a thunderous crash.

Entering Ichabod's cage was different. Despite knowing the roots of it, I had been surprised from the start
by her forceful desire to interact with people. It seemed
impossible to avoid her. I had never been around a socialized eagle before, nor had the other workers at the wildlife centre. The young eagle engaged you completely
when you were in her presence.

In Ichabod's company, my mind was wiped clear of troubles, and I felt refreshed, my whole body relaxed. Whenever I approached the young bird, the weight of her attention felt almost physical. She'd focus her rapier eyes on me, seeming to catalogue the details of my clothes and my face. The location of my hands was of special interest to her. If I was rooting in a pocket absentmindedly, her sharp gaze at the wiggling pocket would draw my attention and still my hand.

I'd seen a similar attentiveness in a dog towards its master. But there was no inherent submission in Ichabod's gaze, no desire to please. Hers was the single-mindedness of a predator. When people were present, she concentrated on them fully. Despite the concerns I had about Ichabod possibly becoming a permanent resident at O.W.L, the sight of the young eagle, her head angled sideways, nut-brown eyes resting calmly on my face, was a welcome respite in a day where every move I made resulted in a negative reaction from the patients.

AS WEEKS TURNED into months, I learned that Ichabod had many moods. One minute the stormy young eagle would hang her head when you appeared, and the next she'd be playfully grabbing at your shoe-laces. Her talons would often appear under the raised door of her cage, grabbing at shadows, sticks or blankets left accidentally nearby. She'd once grabbed part of a quail that way, and since then her clutching talons would appear whenever she heard people approaching.

I crouched once and peered under Ichabod's door, my cheek against the floor. I was rewarded by the sight of the large brown eye of the eagle, who must have laid her own head flat on its side to see under the door. I moved my face fast and, as I'd predicted, her talons appeared next, hoping to hook something.

The volunteers at O.W.L. were unnerved by Ichabod's brazenness. Fewer and fewer people were comfortable entering her cage. As the months passed, the number of people willing to enter dropped to three: a supervisor, an experienced volunteer and me. On days when none of us was working, volunteers would open Ichabod's door, throw the food in and then quickly close the door again. The cleaning of food scraps from the cage was left for us.

One weekend I came to O.W.L. early to spend time with Ichabod before I started the daily chores. She stood on a flat-topped log near the entrance to her cage. Before entering, I gauged her mood by watching her reaction when my face appeared in the door's small barred window. That day, she lifted her head and watched my face with mild interest. As I opened the door, she inclined her head to study my feet, as if watching the white sneakers tread over the green carpet was the most important task in the world. Instead of heading towards the platform I'd planned on cleaning, I eased myself into a crouch,

taking advantage of Ichabod's easygoing mood to settle
on the floor about eight feet away from her. Her talons
gleamed like old ebony against the washed-out wood of
the stump. I knew that if one of them punctured my
skin, the microscopic gristle and bone fragments coating
her talons would add a toxic potency.

Before me, Ichabod slowly opened her wings. I stayed
cautiously still, staring in fascination at the elegant, ten-
sile strength of the large primary feathers, their quills
pushed into the thin covering of skin that lay over the
bones. I thought of the tiny muscles that controlled the
raising, lowering and angling of each individual feather,
and how each of these was part of a whole group of
feathers that, working together, allowed the eagle to fly.

Ichabod opened her wings fully and began to flap,
holding hard to the stump. Each flap sounded like a
loudly expelled breath: huh, huh, huh, huh. Each beat
was faster than the last, yet still she held fast to the
stump. The wind buffeted my face, forcing me to squint.
It was hard not to lean away. If I had been squatting a
foot closer to her, her wings would have brushed my face.

I stretched my cramping legs, then changed to a kneel-
ing position. As I shifted position I could see, through
narrowed eyes, the blurred stroke of wings and sense, in
the downwards flap, their cloaking motion. The fanned air
carried with it Ichabod's scent. It was the essence of eagle,
the scent of all raptors: the faint, copper-sweet smell of

old blood. It always put me in mind of the descriptions I'd read of vampires' breath.

As suddenly as she had started, Ichabod stopped flapping. There was a throbbing to the silence as she settled her wings back against her body, rolling her shoulders from side to side. I opened my eyes wide to see that Ichabod's attitude towards me had changed. From complacency she had switched to curiosity, but the challenging kind. My guts tightened. I didn't know what Ichabod was going to do, but I knew I couldn't rise to my feet in time to protect myself.

At length, Ichabod came to a decision. She shrunk to normal size, and it was then I realized that she had grown taller during our encounter, holding only lightly to the earth in readiness for action. Her eyes softened and feathers lifted all over her body. She shook herself like a dog, and light-grey feather dust was expelled in a cloud that touched the skin of my face. In falconry jargon, I knew that this lifting and shaking of the feathers was called "rousing." Keeping her feathers raised slightly from her body, Ichabod lifted one of her feet, clenched it closed and pulled it up near her body. She made gentle chewing motions with her beak, then closed her eyes.

I sat, spellbound, as the eagle fell asleep before me.

AN EAGLE ON MY ARM

EVERY SATURDAY AT O.W.L., once the volunteers were settled into their jobs and any time-sensitive care, such as medicating a bird, was done, I checked on Ichabod. Even when I was immersed in giving an injection or instructing a volunteer on perch replacement, a small wistful part of me was already out visiting the eagle. Ichabod, now fifteen months old, was entertaining and unpredictable.

One morning I pressed my face against the wooden bars in the window of the door to Ichabod's cage. My eyes went to the flat top of the half wall. It was one of Ichabod's favourite places to eat, and one from which she could watch the door. But she wasn't there today. I looked out to a thick hemlock branch fixed at chest height in the corner of the outside part of the cage. No eagle. Maybe she was close to the door. Ready to ambush me, I thought. I had been "stalked" on several occasions. Shoving my face sideways against the dowels, I peered down at the bright green carpet. Still no eagle. But there was movement, and craning harder, I saw a strange sight. The green carpet was moving. It was growing hills and valleys as an unseen force slowly pushed it up against the wall.

I had finally caught Ichabod in the act of "eagle interior decorating." I had witnessed the results on several occasions, but I had never seen her in action until now. The carpet was sometimes shoved into the centre of the cage; perches and logs were rolled from their usual locations. I'd arrive at the cage to find Ichabod standing on the bare, white-painted concrete—or, more often, on an outside perch, looking as if she had nothing to do with the mess inside.

Today I watched, fascinated, as the carpet moved in fits and starts. Soon the end of a large knobby branch appeared. Five more feet of branch came into view, and then finally the big brown eagle. Ichabod was intent on her task. She held a stout secondary branch in her beak, and she made sideways shoving motions with her head. I wondered if she'd started out simply wanting to move the big branch but it had become twisted in the carpet.

Ichabod hadn't seen me yet, so I remained at the window and continued to observe. Each time she shoved sideways with her head, the eagle stepped into the motion, using her full body weight. Finally, encountering too much resistance, she dropped the smaller branch. The big branch bounced and rolled before settling. Ichabod stood surveying the results. The carpet was wadded against the wall to the left of the door. The large branch lay at a right angle to the wall. Sticking out of the mass of carpet here and there were various small logs and branches that had hitched a ride.

The click of the eagle's talons on the exposed white floor, like unkempt dog nails, drew my eyes back to the perpetrator. Facing away from me, she walked in her rolling pirate's gait to the spot where the half wall met the concrete. Reaching down with her smoky black beak, she rooted in a crack between the floor and the wall. With a quiet croak, she pulled out several strips of piebald rat skin and a pink rat-tail. Gathering these up in one foot, she dropped her wings from her back, spread them like giant fans and lifted into the air. She landed on the half wall, clutching her prizes, and then stood still, as if savouring the thought of the moment when she would begin to demolish her tiny meal.

I backed quietly from the door. At first I was incredulous: all that effort in a well-fed eagle just for a bit of foraging? But it was more likely that, with the crack

revealed by the carpet's absence, Ichabod remembered
finding a previous reward of scraps there, fallen from her
vigorous tearing of carcasses on top of the wall. So why
the "interior decorating" in the first place? The instincts
for play and nest-building combined, with a dose of bore-
dom thrown in? I didn't think I'd ever find out.

Ichabod's private endeavours were a constant source of
fascination for me. I often snuck to her door early in the
day before the noise of volunteers feeding birds and working in surrounding cages disturbed her. I seemed to have
infinite patience for this, often standing in uncomfortable
positions for many minutes until someone came to find
me. It reminded me of the discomfort I'd gladly suffered
one summer at Big Whiteshell Lake as I tried to spot
a bobcat. I'd crouch by the water in the early-morning
hours, my dad's old camera clutched tightly, hoping to
capture the elusive animal on film. As I waited, cold and
cramped, I'd think about passages from Tom Brown Jr.'s
books on stalking wildlife. I'd even taken wind direction
into account. Other times I'd stand in the grey dawn
light spying on great blue herons in the reeds and watching loons through my binoculars until my hands shook
with cold. I'd spend hours watching the pelicans on
the lake, too, marvelling at the accuracy of their forma-
tion flying and at their size as they came to rest on a
submerged rock far across the water. Obviously that fascinated little girl wasn't buried very far under my skin.

One of my most enjoyable rituals with Ichabod was

the cleaning and filling of her pool every week. I even gave the procedure a name, "Killing the green snake," since the green hose became prey for the young eagle. The large plastic wading pool was decorated with cartoon bunny rabbits. For now, the hard pebbled plastic seemed resistant to Ichabod's talons, though I knew that over time replacement pools would have to be found.

I didn't have much time today, so I hoped the cleaning and filling of the pool could be accomplished without much fuss. In preparation, I had collected a thawed rat from the feed room and placed it in a small white bucket near Ichabod's cage door.

As quietly as I could, I pushed the hose through a hole in the chain-link, but my efforts not to attract the eagle's attention were in vain. Ichabod turned immediately to face the chain-link fence, head lowering and wings dropping off her back. Half leaping, half flying, she landed hard on the wooden crosspiece that braced the wall and shuffled along it towards me. I knew what was coming. When she got close enough, the eagle threw up her foot and grasped the hose, yanking on it. I knew better now than to haul back on it. Tug of wars were exciting, and I didn't want to encourage the aggression that came from them. Instead, I left the hose to Ichabod and walked around the back of the care centre to her cage door. On the way I twisted the handle on the water spigot, and the hose jerked as if coming to life. As usual, the sight of the eagle clutching hard to the twitching hose made me laugh. Collecting the small bucket containing her dinner, I unlocked the cage door and stepped inside. Ichabod turned to watch me enter, trying at the same time to hold onto the hose. Water sprayed out from between her toes. When she saw the white bucket, the feathers on the back of her head rose. After a moment's hesitation, she dropped the hose and flew to the half wall.

I set the bucket down by the cage door and walked towards the swinging door set in the half wall. Though this took me directly past the eagle, I knew her attention would be focussed on the bucket, and I hoped that would occupy her long enough for me to clean and rinse the pool. Hidden under my coat was a bristle brush for scrubbing. I knew from past experience that if I carried the brush in plain sight, Ichabod would attempt to steal it at every opportunity.

A whoosh of feathers startled me. I snapped my head up, then relaxed as the eagle opened her wings and dropped to the carpet near the bucket. I dragged more of the hose through the chain-link. The air was crisp, carrying the salty bite of ocean, and for a minute I looked across a farmer's field towards the dyke, seeing the Lilliputian figures of a horse and rider silhouetted in the distance. I felt a pang. *Horses.* I suddenly missed their smooth, veiny skin under my palm, the particular view of the land I'd get only from between their ears.

I was still lost in thought when a clattering sound came from behind me. Chiding myself for daydreaming in an eagle's cage, I spun around. Ichabod swayed drunkenly back and forth by the door, the bucket overturned on her head.

Laughter bubbled up in me. I put the hose and brush down and walked towards the careening eagle. She backed into my legs before switching direction and hitting the wall. As I lifted the bucket from her head, I saw that she held the rat firmly in her beak. The absurdity of the sight made me laugh again. Affronted, Ichabod hopped away, opened her wings and flew onto the half wall. She paused there only briefly before flying to the hemlock perch with her hard-won quarry. I scrubbed and filled her pool without further incident.

That evening, still laughing at the memory of Ichabod with a bucket on her head, I told the story to my boyfriend, Todd. We'd been dating for a while and had recently moved in together. He smiled, then asked if I would give O.W.L. a miss the following weekend, complaining that I seldom spent weekend time with him. Tamping down the feeling of panic that arose at the thought of missing even one shift at O.W.L.—and with Ichabod—I gave a noncommittal response.

As the weekend drew nearer, my tension grew. I couldn't concentrate on my coursework, and Todd and I argued in the evenings. I tried to explain what my work at O.W. L. meant to me, using the example of an injured eagle that had been admitted to the centre the weekend before. Searching the new patient to uncover a reason for his mysterious drooping wing and injured leg, I had discovered the entry and exit points of the electric shock he'd received. Todd responded with the jab that I cared more about the birds at O.W. L. than I did about anything else, including him. I allowed myself to contemplate a weekend without O.W. L. I knew that the volunteers would feed Ichabod, and someone would probably stop outside the chain-link to talk with her as they walked by. She'd be fine, I thought. Then it struck me: I wouldn't. My guilt and insecurity were no match for the deep need I knew only the birds at O.W. L. could meet. My voice shaking, I told Todd that I would definitely be going to the centre that weekend. He stormed out in anger.

Alone in our apartment, I couldn't sleep. A desperation bordering on the fanatical gripped me when I thought of my life without my work at O.W. L. A lump of fear jammed my throat. I sat up, trying to swallow. After gulping cool, deep breaths of night air, I closed my eyes and lay down again, arms hugging my ribs. A jumbled mix of sensations washed over me: the sound of an eagle's wing cutting a swath through the air, the muted clop of hooves on distant pavement, the wobble of a dead owl's head as I carefully lifted him from his cage. As I slipped into the hazy world of almost-sleep, I imagined sliding my hand into my heavy eagle glove. The glove fingers were bent into predetermined shapes. At first my fingers resisted the channels made for them, then they gave in to the cant of thumb, the curl of index and ring fingers. Suddenly, I was in Ichabod's cage. I stretched my gloved arm out from my body, opening the angle at the crook of my elbow. Ichabod stood before me, eyes hard and bright as diamonds.

I opened my eyes, confused to see the familiar shadowed shape of lamp and bedside table. Just a dream, I told myself. Though I felt the eagle's presence strongly, I resisted the urge to scan the room for her. I unfolded my arms one at a time, leaving my palms open to the air. I fell asleep like that, arms flung out like wings.

GLOVES WERE an essential piece of equipment when handling raptors. At O.W.L., we used them mostly in the day-to-day moving of raptors from one cage to another. The trade-off between protection and dexterity was most noticeable in our work with small hawks and owls. Slender leather gloves did not protect our hands from the thin talons of sharp-shinned hawks or those of the tiny falcons called kestrels. Yet the flexibility these gloves allowed meant you could hold a narrow body with its thundering heart firmly and gently while medicated eyedrops were administered or an infected foot was soaked.

Thin leather gloves were also the gloves of choice

when catching small owls, such as the yellow-eyed western screech owl, which at seven to ten inches in height was a smaller version of the great horned owl. The seven-to-eight-inch northern saw-whet owl, with its tawny striped plumage, and the diminutive but fierce northern pygmy owl, of six-to-seven-inch stature, were also caught with these lightweight gloves.

Wrist-length welder's gloves of soft grey suede protected our hands from the ghostly, monkey-faced common barn owl, fourteen to twenty inches in height, and the grey-striped barred owl, with its navy eyes and seventeen-to-twenty-four-inch height. The Cooper's hawk, thin-legged and crow-sized, could be caught with either thin leather gloves or welder's gloves, depending on the volunteer's preference. Northern harriers, narrow-bodied hawks with long wings and tail, sometimes called marsh hawks, had small feet that could also be handled with the welder's gloves.

The thickest gloves, wrist-length and made of cowhide, were reserved for the birds with the strongest feet. The red-tailed hawk, a chunky, broad-winged hawk of twenty-one to twenty-five inches, had short, powerful toes and thick talons. Work with snowy owls, which ranged in height from twenty to twenty-seven inches, called for the extra protection of the cowhide gloves, as did work with great horned owls, arguably the most powerful birds of prey for their size.

At first we used cowhide gloves for both types of eagles at the wildlife centre, golden and bald. The gloves were worn in conjunction with a heavy jacket, since the wide stance of an eagle, with feet the size of a human hand, meant that the bird had immense reach and power. Sometimes an eagle would throw out a foot, grabbing a volunteer's forearm. I had a round puncture scar on my own forearm from the day we'd released Chatty Kathy. After a time, the centre began to order special forearm-length eagle gloves.

Normally gloves were worn when catching birds to move them from cage to cage or when handling the educational birds. However, because Ichabod had invaded my space the last few times I'd cleaned her pool, I'd started wearing one of these gloves in her cage for protection. She'd snuck up on me while I was scrubbing one day and grabbed the heel of my running shoe. My startled exclamation had spooked her into letting go. Another time, she'd leapt onto the edge of the wading pool as I cleaned it and grabbed at the hand holding the scrub brush, missing narrowly. She then moved to a vantage point three feet away from which she glared at me, her demeanour changed from playful to dangerous in a split second. I counted myself lucky when the noise of volunteers talking in a neighbouring cage distracted her. For these reasons, the number of people willing to enter Ichabod's cage had now dropped to two: myself and the other supervisor. The experienced volunteer had decided to stop one day when Ichabod leapt at her face. The other supervisor now wore a glove whenever she entered Ichabod's cage, too.

Because I was already wearing a glove in Ichabod's cage, it seemed logical to invite her to stand on it. Having seen falconers with their mannerly birds sitting on their arms, I began introducing the glove to Ichabod, inviting her at first just to touch it. Her initial reaction was to chitter nervously as the glove approached and move away, assuming it meant she was about to be caught. After a while, emboldened by my arm's leather casing, I took to standing a foot away from her with my arm held out. Ichabod was so caught up in looking at the glove that I felt no vibes of aggression. She began to reach out hesitantly with her foot towards the glove. Each time I'd hold my breath, sure she was going to step completely on the glove, but she'd subside again to her perch. It got so that during the course of a shift at O.W.L., I'd reenter her cage several times and casually offer the glove. In our third session one day, she placed a foot tentatively on the leather and left it there.

My next weekend day, when I approached the eagle with the glove, she slapped it with her foot, chattering loudly. Finally, after five minutes of my waiting, she placed one foot on the glove, hesitated, and then stepped on with both feet. Quickly, I rested my hand on the perch she had stepped from to steady my arm under the unaccustomed weight. Ichabod's head reared back to the height of mine. She looked into the distance through the chain-link and made a quiet croaking sound. My heart pounding, I stood for the first time with an eagle on my arm, oriented towards the ocean, looking with her over the fields.

ONE DAY during my shift, I went to the medical room to look at Ichabod's case card. I was unable to find it at first, but I finally located it in the section marked "Non-releasable." Almost two years into Ichabod's stay at O.W. L., the centre's director had made the decision I was dreading. I stood, frozen, the card in my hand. With every injured bird at O.W. L., I pictured the moment of release, the time when my hands would let go of the body and the wind from churning wings would blow against my face. I had held hard to this vision for Ichabod, too. As I thought of her contained in a cage, her big wings restricted from truly stretching out, a lump formed in my throat. Then the glimmer of an outrageous idea surfaced in my mind. The only birds in captivity that seemed content were falconers' birds. They flew as nature intended, then retired to an enclosure. The word that best seemed to describe their attitude after a hunting flight was "satiated." I shelved the thought almost immediately, though, my gut churning at the thought of Ichabod permanently in a cage.

After a few minutes, I realized I felt the need to
see Lucy, the red-tailed hawk, who resided in the non-
releasable cages outside. Lucy had been socialized to
people at a young age, when it was discovered she had a
breathing problem from pesticide poisoning. Despite
her socialization, she had retained her sense of identity as
a red-tailed hawk and depicted no characteristic imprint
behaviours, such as protection of her food from people
or aggression.

Lucy stood on a perch in her cage, buff-coloured
chest wide and expanded, brown head thrown back as she
eyed the sky for other red-tails. "Luce," I said softly, using
my nickname for her. She looked at me with her special
blend of curiosity and kindness. I'd never thought
of kindness as an adjective that could describe a bird of
prey; I would have ridiculed the observation, in fact, had
I heard it before I met Lucy. Lucy had sat gently many
times on my bare arm, her sharp talons stretching the
skin of my wrist but leaving not a scratch. She was handled by a myriad of volunteers and was a veteran of many
educational fairs. Sometimes, she decided to avoid the
glove of the volunteer who had come to place her in a
crate for transport. She'd wait until the person was inches
away, then elegantly fly to a perch behind the volunteer,
turning back expectantly to wait for the next approach.
On a few occasions, I'd been sent in to help. I'd stand in
the middle of Lucy's cage for a minute or two and then

speak to her. I'd walk towards her until my arm was within inches of her feet. She'd pause, then step onto the glove. Her compliance seemed co-operative in these instances rather than forced.

Today I stood beyond the chain-link, looking to Lucy for solace. I needed something to ease the ache that had started when I read Ichabod's case card. The little red-tailed hawk turned her head sideways, one eye scanning the patchy blue sky above. Her beak opened, and she let out a yip. I strained my eyes to see what she did. A bird no bigger than a dot circled high above. Lucy opened her beak and let out a series of calls: *keer, keer.* A faint answer came back, and Lucy stood up straighter and called again, her voice raspier and more nasal. The hawk above answered once.

Lucy angled her head back to level, lifted all her feathers like a giant feather duster and shook her body before settling her feathers back against her skin. She swished her tail crisply back and forth three times. I recognized the body language from Ichabod. It seemed a sort of settling and relaxing, a letting in of air under the feathers. The swishing of the tail seemed almost insolent. Lucy lifted one foot up until it disappeared into her body feathers. I glanced around to see if anyone was looking and then shook myself like a dog, releasing some of the tension in my body, my throat working easier now.

8

"UP! UP!"

THE FIRST TIME I ever saw a falconer,
I was walking from O.W.L. to the bus
stop. I noticed a man standing near the junction of the
road; he had something on his arm, but I wasn't sure
what. As I approached, I noticed that his elbow was bent
and held slightly away from his body. A black leather
glove encased his hand and wrist, and on it stood a tall,
lean hawk.

I stepped from the shoulder of the road towards the
pair, but the man turned and began walking along one of
the roads that led to the old airport, swinging a stout
branch in his free hand. The late sun was in front of him,
providing me with a striking silhouette of man and

hawk. I thought about following them, but there was something private about the scene, a kind of communion between two beings. From the little I knew of falconry, I figured that, once deep into the old airport area, the man would unclip the leash from the hawk's jesses, the soft leather straps hanging from the bird's legs, and set the bird free. The branch in his hands would likely be used to drive rabbits from the brambles for the hawk to kill. As I watched them walking into the distance, I could see the man's head and the hawk's inclined towards one another, as if they were conversing.

I'd never heard of anyone doing falconry with a bald eagle, but my crazy dream of working with Ichabod like this refused to go away. I was still enrolled in some courses at the university, but the young eagle to which I'd become so attached occupied my mind more and more.

One Saturday, I shrugged on the camouflage jacket that had become my eagle-feeding uniform. As I walked out the back door of the care centre towards Ichabod's cage, I pulled the elbow-length eagle glove onto my left hand and arm. Patting the deep chest pocket of my jacket, I double-checked my supply of dead baby mice, which we called "pinkies." Underneath the baby mice were the several large rat pieces that comprised Ichabod's daily feeding.

As I unlocked the cage door, I peeked through the barred window, locating the young eagle on the rough-barked Douglas fir branch I'd recently nailed up. While I watched, she hopscotched, with a lazy unfolding of her wings, to the half wall closer to the door. Her long legs swung forward as she landed. As I pulled the door open, she chirred softly in a friendly manner.

Ichabod was two years old now. Her eyes were wood-brown, her head feathers shot through with a small amount of white. She opened her black beak, exposing its pale pink insides, and croaked three times. I spoke quietly as I walked towards her. I watched carefully for telltale signs of aggression, such as the raising of her head feathers or the lifting of her beak, but there was nothing. Ichabod watched me with mild interest, her eyes almost cocker-spaniel-like.

When I was a couple of feet away, I turned my back and stretched out my left gloved arm. Ichabod reached out with one foot tentatively. I waited. I had deliberately placed myself too far from the wall for her to be com-fortable with one leg extended. She withdrew her foot. Looking over my shoulder, I saw certainty take over her body like a live current, snapping her up straighter. She jumped and landed on the glove with enough force to rock my arm. I stepped towards the wall, resting my hand there to steady it. The eagle reared her head back and let loose a throaty croak of triumph. I winced as she clenched and unclenched her feet. I was concerned about her right foot, the one closest to my body. She was standing very wide, and her right foot was holding hard to the edge of my glove at the elbow. I could feel the bruising pinch of her talons, but there was no puncture yet, since her talons were twisted into the bunched jacket at my elbow. I raised my gloved hand higher, in a move I'd seen falconers perform. Raptors tended to want to sit at the highest point of the glove, in this case my hand. I released a quiet sigh of relief as Ichabod extricated herself from my jacket and shifted up the glove towards my hand, her right foot landing mid-forearm.

As I reached into my chest pocket, I watched her eyes sharpen. Pulling out a single baby mouse, I held it towards her beak. This had become part of our routine while Ichabod stood on the glove, and I observed her as she transformed again. The fierce predator that had leapt on my arm with such gusto now turned her head sideways and chattered softly at the mouse as she took it with utmost delicacy from my outstretched fingers. My fingertips brushed the hard shell of her beak. I looked down at her lowered head, listening to the breathy chatter she emitted continuously from her half-open beak like gossipy prattle. As I held out another pinkie, a cold wash of ocean air hit my nostrils. The light in the cage had a peculiar clarity, edging the tiny feathers on Ichabod's head with silver. The young eagle's touching of my fingertips had enchanted me, drawing a spell around me as surely as any magician in a fairytale.

ICHABOD'S TENDENCY these days was to grab new objects with her feet, then reach down and worry them with her giant beak. She'd grab at the trailing drawstrings on my jacket and attempt to take them up to her platform, the place many of her new interests wound up. I'd learned to check my clothing before I entered her cage: no zippers flapping open, no boots with long laces and definitely no dangling earrings. I'd once worn shiny gold flying hawk earrings to O.W.L. and narrowly missed having them ripped off by Oddey, the barn owl, as he sat on my shoulder during a tour.

One morning I watched the eagle snatch the rat I'd thrown her from the air with a precise movement and then, within the same fluid moment, lift to the half wall, her prize firmly gripped in one foot. She flexed her toes and punched her talons into the rat's skin. I winced a little at the ease with which she punctured the piebald fur. Despite her gentleness when taking pinkies from my fingers, Ichabod was all business about her quotient of rats.

Today, the eagle shifted a quarter turn from the cage door as I opened it, lowered her head and glared at me. I laughed but refused to be driven from my vantage point. "Cranky girl," I said. At the sound of my voice, she glowered.

Ichabod's brown wings looked thick and heavy over her back as she stood on the half wall. Suddenly she straightened, lifted her head and dropped her shoulders.

She drew the tips of her wings towards her feet, fanning out her feathers to conceal her food from me. This was called "mantling," I knew. She looked like a diva onstage, cloak pulled around her for dramatic effect. The bird's head, held high, seemed small at the end of her out-stretched neck. I'd also seen her mantle from wild hawks and eagles flying above her cage.

Ichabod had to lower her head to eat, though she kept her wings drawn around her feet. She repositioned the rat, talons from both feet pinning it to the wood, then pulled upwards on the rat's body with her beak, rip-ping away a strip with an ease that was chilling. She tore and swallowed, tore and swallowed. Sometimes, remem-bering her audience, she would jerk her head briefly in my direction, her eyes crackling with possessive fire.

I had developed a system of cleaning Ichabod's cage while she ate, removing scraps of food from the previous day. At first it had made no difference when I performed this duty. But she had begun to enter my body space more and more often as she matured. Now I timed my cleaning sprees to coincide with her mealtimes. The sounds of the eagle eating relaxed me. I welcomed the macabre crunch of bone and gristle along with a sound like that of heavy paper being torn as Ichabod ripped long strips from the dead rat she clutched in her talons. She had never left her food to attack me.

If I tried to move around the eagle's cage when she

wasn't eating, though, I'd often find myself confronting Ichabod as she blocked my path to a particular log or stump. Without making a conscious decision to do so, I started to cluck at her, using the classic "move along" command taught to horses. The sound came naturally from all the riding I'd done as a teenager. Sometimes I would even hear myself clucking at people in crowds to encourage them to move faster. So it seemed natural to cluck at the eagle too. Surprisingly, the technique was successful: Ichabod began to respond consistently whenever I clucked. I was puzzled about why this was. She received no food for obeying my command. Perhaps it related to the social nature of bald eagles. Whatever the reason, when I clucked, pointed and said "Move," the eagle responded more often than not. Even when she didn't, it seemed that she understood what I wanted but chose to defy me.

The educational birds that were tame enough to be presented to a crowd wore leather jesses around their lower legs. A leather leash was attached to these by clipping it through slits in the ends of the jesses. If a jessed bird tried to fly off the glove—or, in falconry parlance, "bate"—the jesses stopped it short. The straps also kept the bird from wandering up the glove or, in Oddey's case, since he rode on volunteers' shoulders, from jumping onto volunteers' heads, as he was inclined to do. Oddey and Lucy wore jesses at all times, since they did the bulk of the educational work.

Ichabod had been jessed briefly at a young age by
a falconer, but she'd worried at the straps with her beak
until, days later, they were off. She wore no jesses around
her legs now, and both falconers and volunteers thought
I was crazy to work with an unrestrained eagle on the
glove. I'd heard tales of eagles grabbing at people's necks
and faces with their giant feet, but that didn't stop me.
Either luck or something in the nature of the young
eagle kept this danger at bay. At least for now, though
completely unrestrained, Ichabod stood in a mannerly
way on the glove while being fed tidbits.

I NOTICED different details in Ichabod's plumage in
different types of light. In bright sunlight, she looked
glossy. Overcast days gave her feathers a matte look, and
the bird herself a brooding presence. I seemed to see
a different eagle every time I looked.

One windy, cloudy Saturday I paused to watch Ichabod through her cage door. The short feathers on her
body stood out in sharp relief against the long quills.
She appeared to be made of brown scales, with even her
wings taking on a brittle, elongated look. The eagle stood
on a branch in the outside part of her cage, snowcapped
Mount Baker behind her. Although the mountain
was many miles away, across the border in Washington
state, it often seemed close. Today, rafts of clouds hovered
around the mountain's base. The peak's white hood
reminded me of the head of an adult bald eagle.

Ichabod's head still had only a small amount of white shot through it. It would be another four years before she was completely white-headed. Two dark-brown strips led back from her eyes on each side of her head, making her look like a bandit. Her beak was grey from arch to tip, but there was a hint of pale lemon from the nares, or nostrils, back towards her head. This was the harbinger of the yellow beak to come. Her eyes were still brown, though they would soon begin to turn yellow at the same pace as her beak.

Ichabod was facing the door of her cage, but she seemed oblivious to me. I stood where I was for a minute, breathing deeply. The salty scent of the ocean tinged the air, and I could hear, in the distance, the rhythmical clacking of a coal train on its way east.

I cupped my pocket, which held a medium-sized rat along with twenty or so pinkies. As I slid the key into the small gold lock on the cage door, Ichabod's head whipped towards me, and she dropped her wings from her body. She tilted her head abruptly sideways, one eye skyward. I looked up, but I couldn't see what transfixed her. Slipping the elbow-length eagle glove onto my left arm, I slid the lock free, pulled the door open and stepped inside. As I walked out of the indoor area onto the grass, Ichabod glanced at me, then returned her attention to the sky. I scanned it myself, and after a moment caught sight of a large bird slipping through the thin mist of clouds

around a patch of blue. Ichabod let out a yip. Then
suddenly there were two birds in the sky, one above the
other. As they moved into the widening patch of blue,
even I, with my less acute vision, could see they were two
adult eagles. Instinctively I moved closer to Ichabod, as
people do when pointing something out to one another.
I was only about five feet away from where the young
bird perched on her favourite hemlock branch.

The eagles circled in the patch of blue, one still
slightly above the other. Then the bird below pulled in its
wings and dropped in a long, gradual line down through
the clouds. It faded from view as the clouds thickened.
The other eagle continued its slow, wide circle, exquisitely
alone in the curved bowl of sky. Minutes passed, and it
seemed the eagle would lazily traverse this piece of sky
forever. Then its wings folded and the eagle dropped alti-
tude, flying like a grey ghost in the thin clouds before
disappearing.

I jumped when Ichabod let out a harsh croak. Instantly
it came home to me that I had been bird-watching with
an eagle only a few feet away. As I looked at her, I felt
the odd combination of thrill and fear with which I was
becoming so familiar. She glared back at me, every feather
on her head erect, bony brow over burning eyes giving
the distinct impression of a frown.

I stood frozen, as prey has for centuries under such
a gaze. My hand opened and closed involuntarily, perhaps

instinctively, craving a weapon or a shield. The small
movement drew Ichabod's eyes for a second, then she
returned her gaze to my face. She began to step along her
perch towards me, hissing like a snake. She dropped the
wings off her back, her head even with mine. Now she
was less than three feet away.

I knew what could happen, yet I was relaxed and
still. My eyes took in the eagle's incredible presence, the
breadth of her chest, her thick legs firmly holding to
the branch. I felt alive and light on my feet, as if I were
ready for anything.

Almost without thinking about it, I turned away
from the eagle, slipping my right hand into the pocket
laden with mice. As I did so, I thrust out my gloved
left arm and said sharply, "Up! Up!"

Ichabod leapt at me before my arm was fully straightened, her legs swinging forward. As she landed squarely
on the glove, I felt relief course through me in waves.
She clenched hard, then relaxed her grip. I pulled a baby
mouse from my pocket, and her talons gripped my
leather-clad arm in response. Carefully, holding it by
the rear end with the tips of my fingers, I held the pinkie
up to her beak.

Ichabod reached forward quickly. I almost flinched
but manage to control it. She paused, beak inches from
my fingers. Then she turned her head sideways and delicately extricated the morsel, her beak not even brushing
my skin. I reached for another tidbit.

AS TIME WENT BY, I was more and more often the unwilling participant in eagle games involving stealth and attack. Sometimes Ichabod was territorial about her cage or a specific perch in it, and then the element of play disappeared completely. One day as I was cleaning her pool, she struck out at me with a foot, piercing the back of my right hand through my rubber glove. I dropped the scrub brush I'd been holding and she bore it off in triumph, leaving me with a deeply cut hand to nurse.

I seemed to be developing heightened peripheral vision. Once, as I crouched cleaning Ichabod's pool, I leapt backwards and landed in a heap after seeing a loose feather twirling in the wind at the edge of my vision.

Branches and stumps dropped off by the public were piled in a heap outside the care centre. O.W.L.'s director had also intercepted more than one truck laden with branches on its way to the nearby dump. When setting up cages or replacing perches, we rooted through this pile. I'd found various unusual-shaped stumps and branches, and Ichabod had a collection of them in the indoor portion of her cage. I regularly placed her food on the broad end of a stump about a foot and a half in height.

Ichabod would amble along the ground towards me, stop ten feet away, then rush quickly at my legs and grab my foot. She enjoyed this manoeuvre even more if I was moving. Then she'd make a charge at my feet, crowing a triumphant creaky call when she caught one. One day

I caught her looking up at me speculatively, head cocked sideways as if to say, "Yeah, I think I can take ya."

By accident, I discovered that my nerves improved when I held a branch in my hand. Then I became a primate with a weapon. The psychological effect of protecting myself had a profound result on my body language, and Ichabod initiated aggressive confrontations less frequently.

I needed to find a way to teach the eagle to respect my space. The supervisor who entered Ichabod's cage during the week suggested I try using a mop. The idea sounded odd, but the more I thought about it, the more it appealed to me. Rather than considering the mop as a weapon, I saw it as a blocking device or a shield. I had no idea what an eagle would think of a human with a mop. I was about to find out.

9

MOP IN HAND

THE MOPS AT O.W.L. hung on a rack outside the back door. "Choose your weapon," I muttered to myself as I stood before them one weekend morning. The hammering of the rain on the metal roof became white noise as I stood there deliberating. Finally I chose the one with the shaggiest head and the smallest circumference of handle. I hefted it in my hand. Housework was definitely not my forte; holding a mop was unusual for me.

Eager to see how Ichabod would react, I headed straight for her cage. I undid the lock, stepped in, closed the door behind me and then stood uncertainly for a moment, grasping the mop in my right hand. Where was she? Sheets of rain made it difficult to see the perches in the outside part of the cage, but then I caught the outline of the eagle on a corner perch. Ichabod opened her wings. The big branch creaked as she bounced into the air, and my view was filled with eagle as she flew in my direction. Expecting her to land on the half wall, I was unprepared when she continued towards me.

"HEY!" I yelled in surprise and fear. The bird dropped abruptly and landed on the carpet about eight feet away, skidding slightly. I held still, brandishing the mop in front of me. The eagle peered up at me with bright eyes. She lowered her head and shook herself, spraying droplets of water over my legs. Her feathers, their waterproofing oil coming from the preen gland at the base of her tail, appeared miraculously dry despite the weather. The rain beaded on them, then rolled off.

Ichabod opened her wings, shook herself once more and then sidled towards me.

"HEY!" I shouted again. One scaly yellow foot shot out and grabbed the laced top of my sneakers. I yanked my foot backwards. The eagle opened her wings, raised the crest of feathers at the back of her head and grabbed my ankle.

"Ahhh!" The cry escaped my lips as I felt the white-hot pain of a talon penetrate my sock. The mop, I remembered suddenly. I shoved the mop head down between the eagle's head and my lower thigh.

Now it was Ichabod's turn to be surprised. With a squeak, she let go of my ankle and grabbed the dread-locks of the mop with one foot, clutching my sneaker with the other. I hauled up on the mop to break her hold. She stretched between the shoe and the mop at first, then let go of my sneaker, her free foot swinging up to join the one entwined in the mop head. Suddenly I recognized a new danger. The mop and eagle were waist-level now—and much closer to my face.

I shoved the head of the mop down dramatically and stepped back. With a frustrated shriek, Ichabod let go of it and landed in an ungainly heap on the ground. I stepped back further. She righted herself, then dropped her head, from there lifting her beak high. Her eyes glit-tered. I stepped sideways, not wanting to display any action she would consider weakness. "Easy there, settle down now," I murmured. This bird was almost unrecog-nizable as the eagle who gently extracted pinkies from my fingers.

Ichabod and I stood in our respective spots at an impasse. Then, after some of the longest minutes of my life, her crest slowly dropped. She drew a wing forward and, selecting one long brown flight feather, ran her beak along it, knitting together imaginary damage to the tiny feather barbules with her beak. Grooming herself to "save face"? I couldn't be sure. Maybe she had just decided that it was time to attend to her feathers. I stepped sideways again and then, in a roundabout way, hobbled to the door, diminishing my limp as best I could in my own version of saving face. As I backed out, I watched the eagle begin what looked like a protracted grooming session.

I locked the cage door and headed for the medical room in search of peroxide. I knew without looking that I had a gash, possibly even a bad puncture, in the skin on my ankle. There was a neat round hole through my sock, its edges crusted with blood. When I removed my sock, I discovered a small puncture. By that evening, my ankle was swollen. I wasn't too worried, though. My tetanus shot was up-to-date. I also had a good immune system, I knew, bolstered by the fact that I was grabbed often enough by birds of prey to allow me to build some immunity against dirty talons. People working with snakes experienced the same toughening of the immune system, I'd heard.

THE NEXT THREE TIMES I brought the mop into the cage, Ichabod ignored it completely. One afternoon I decided to clean the outdoor part of her cage while she devoured, with characteristic gusto, half a rabbit. Rabbits were not a regular dinner entree, so I knew she'd eat every scrap. As I worked, small sparrows flitted in and out of the cage through the chain-link, ignored by Ichabod. Starlings often flew into the cage too, making their rusty-hinge cry. The far-off scree of a red-tailed hawk sounded from somewhere far above, and I heard Lucy's distinctive hoarse reply from the educational cages.

I scanned the ground, searching for white and black scraps of rat. Scraping the outside platform with rubber-gloved fingers, I removed the remains of recent meals along with shrivelled bits missed in earlier cleanings. At one point, I leaned the mop against the platform so that I could clean with both hands. I was ten feet away before I remembered it. I tensed as I turned to retrieve it, then relaxed when I heard a ripping sound and the pop of a rabbit bone breaking. A fetid smell assailed my nostrils. Ichabod must have pierced the rabbit's bowel. Lovely.

A song sparrow trilled from a fencepost nearby, the buzzy bright notes changing to a liquid melody so clear it sent a shiver through me. For a moment, I had a deep awareness of the immensity of the natural world, in which the sparrow and I played our tiny parts. I had the sense of clinging to a shoreline, to the edge of a continent. The pungent aroma of mud flats laced with salt was an omnipresent reminder of the ocean half a mile away. I wondered if Ichabod knew there was water close by, even though she couldn't see it. The sense of smell in many birds of prey—and in birds in general—is poorly developed, sometimes even absent, though vultures and scavenger birds can smell. I wasn't sure about eagles.

I heard a whoosh and looked up quickly. The eagle was already in the air halfway towards me. "Damn it!"

I yelled, mad at myself for not watching her. As if in slow motion, I saw her "landing gear" drop, thick legs swinging down, large taloned feet transformed into claws. Then I noticed her eyes: they were rivetted on the mop. My breathing deepened. My heart, which had been pounding like a trip-hammer, slowed down, and I could

hear the rhythmic beating of blood in my ears under the rush of wind from giant wings. My muscles felt re-laxed and ready. Ichabod was one wing beat away from landing when I stepped towards her and shoved the mop head into her stomach. She couldn't raise her legs above it, and she let out a whimper of frustration. She braked with her tail fanned out, then tucked in her wings slightly, turned in the air and flew back to a perch.

Seeing the acrobatic ease of her turn, I was surprised the eagle hadn't countered my move. Never under-estimate the element of surprise, I thought. I let out a shaky breath. Every nerve was alive and tingling. I could feel the blood pumping through my index finger where it rested against the mop. I walked from the cage, exhausted.

SOMETIMES WHEN I cleaned Ichabod's cage I'd see a horse and rider galloping along the distant dyke, look-ing like toy figurines held up to the horizon. I'd heard recently that there was a riding facility close to where I lived, and one afternoon I resolved to check it out.

The stable's three barns were nestled in the forest of Burnaby Lake Park. I walked through the wide aisles, listening to the familiar sounds of horses munching hay, eyeing the silken-headed creatures I'd missed so much. Down a shady trail were two outside riding rings. I asked a man exercising a fiery dark-brown horse if he knew of any horses to lease and discovered he had one that needed a rider. As I made arrangements to meet Annie, the chestnut thoroughbred mare he spoke of, excitement coursed through me. Back into horses!

Days later I stood near a fenced ring watching a marmalade-coloured horse gallop loose. Dust spurted from under his hooves, hazing his outline as he charged along the fence line. A seal-brown horse was added to the ring. The first horse greeted the second with a mincing trot and arched neck. Tails lifted like banners, the two ran the length of the ring together before subsiding to a walk, noses wuffling the dirt. Then both horses rolled on the ground, wriggling itchy backs into the bark-mulch surface.

I drank in the sight of these exquisite creatures. Standing there, I thought about how I felt reintroduced to the world whenever I let myself into the sensory life of a bird or an animal. Like eagles, horses knew the truth about you. They picked up on the feelings that lay beneath the surface. Horses were definitely easier and more welcoming than eagles, though. I walked back to the barn to ready Annie for our ride.

BY NOW, I was the only person left at O.W.L. who was willing to work with Ichabod. The other supervisor had stopped working at the centre. Food was thrown into Ichabod's cage during the week, and I did a thorough job of cleaning up the food remains on the weekends. Nonetheless, whenever the wildlife centre's director asked me questions about Ichabod, I felt a sense of panic. I knew some people wondered what purpose there was for this non-releasable eagle at the centre. Some saw her as a liability, I knew. I recognized how important the eagle had become to me, but I didn't know how to articulate that without sounding selfish. I was also fairly sure that I could train the bird to do educational work in some way. Nonetheless, I feared getting more deeply attached to Ichabod, afraid she'd be taken away from me, afraid I'd fail. I started spending more and more time at the barn with the horses. One weekend, for the first time in over a year, I cancelled my shift at O.W.L., making arrangements for a volunteer to throw Ichabod's food in through her cage door.

I went to the barn early that Saturday morning, deliberately pushing away all thoughts of the early-morning routine at O.W.L. The raised bark-mulch paths leading from the barns to the park trails were dry, but the surrounding bog lent a faint smell of decay to the air.

I stood in front of Annie's stall and looked at the big chestnut mare. Her huge brown eyes and wide white blaze gave her a perpetually startled look. Lifting her halter and lead rope from the hook on the door, I approached her quietly. Because Annie was head-shy—nervous of people reaching for her head and ears—I slowed my breathing, calming myself so as not to alarm her. She had started her life as a prospective racehorse, and I knew that something had happened at the racetrack to give her this fear. A shudder went through Annie's big body when she saw me. It seemed to be a sigh of relief. *Oh, it's you,* I imagined her saying. Not for the first time, I wondered about the sensitivity of horses to body language. It bordered on the telepathic. Several times I'd tensed while leading Annie, and she had thrown her head and pranced to the end of the lead rope. Now I rubbed her forehead and slipped the halter gently over her head. Sliding a strap behind her ears with care, I buckled the halter near her left temple. Her fear was less each time I came, and I hoped that one day she would trust me completely. I took Annie's saddle, bridle and brushes from the locked cupboard where they were stored and readied the mare for our trail ride.

The rhythm of Annie's long strides soothed me as we walked past the riding rings towards the trails. Some ducks exploded out of a ditch, and the mare leapt sideways. Firmly ensconced in the saddle, I moved as if part of her, my body shifting with hers. I was a bit rusty after not riding for years, but over the past few months I had discovered how much my body remembered. My balance was still there.

A high-pitched noise sounded above the trees, and Annie raised her head with mine. An adult red-tailed hawk circled in the flawless blue of the sky, each tail feather articulated crisply in a large fan. Annie reached for an overhanging branch to munch leaves while I craned my neck to keep the hawk in sight. I wondered what Ichabod was doing. Did eagles have a sense of time? Would she realize that it was time for me to come and wonder where I was? Would she be bored and unsettled when left alone in her cage? Guilt washed over me. I should be at O.W.L. The pools in the educational birds' cages needed cleaning this weekend, as did those of many of the recuperating residents. Ichabod's pool was due for a scrubbing too, though I knew no one would venture to do it. I shivered, causing Annie to step forward uncertainly. I placated her with a stroke along her shoulder.

That night, I dreamed of the wind slapping my cheeks as I stood in the eagle's cage. My eyelashes were jewelled with sunlight, and for a moment Ichabod herself was surrounded by chips of brilliance. Then an enormous cloud snuffed out the sun. The eagle now stood much farther away, dark and distant, and the fields that had been so golden and alive with promise behind her now seemed merely drab farmland. I awoke suddenly, confused for a moment that the sky was still dark. My eyelashes were spiked with teardrops, and there was a tight feeling in my throat.

ROYAL-BLUE AND RED banners hung from the pillars along the glass-roofed quadrangle of Simon Fraser University. Haunting notes from bagpipes lingered in the air. I was graduating from university with a B.A. in geography. With my student loans running out, I had decided to graduate now, but I hoped to find funds in the future to return and finish a biology degree. In the meantime, I had to find a job. I was sorry to be leaving school. My mind had been stretched and opened to new ideas. I had learned how to research and write papers on almost anything, and I had found myself following interesting tangents much of the time. I worried that a paying job wouldn't provide the same stimulus.

After weeks of looking, I found a summer job as a secretary in the steward's office at the local racetrack. The tasks were repetitive, but the building where I worked was surrounded by horses. There were no windows in the office, but if I listened hard enough, I could hear the clatter of shod hooves on pavement. Whenever I could sneak out, I watched the horses run, my heart in my throat. But those moments were few and far between. Most of the time a dull feeling suffused me, and the façade of cheerfulness the office required was difficult to keep up.

In my battered Chevy Caprice, I made my way out to
O.W. L. on the weekends, accompanied on the trip by the
spiders that lived in the cracked dashboard. I drove on
automatic pilot, turning the wheel at the appropriate
places, braking when the situation called for it. Once I
was inside O.W. L., though, my lethargy usually lessened.

As I entered the wildlife centre one morning, I heard
a ruckus in the intensive care room. I opened the door
to hear a voice hissing, "Shut the door, quick!" I pulled it
closed behind me as I slipped into the room. When she
saw me, the volunteer inside passed a hand over her forehead, as if wiping away sweat. With her chin she directed
my eyes to the top of a stack of large dog kennels. There
stood a small brown hawk. The bird's body vibrated with
intensity. His mustard-coloured eyes darted around the
room. He was tiny, maybe eleven inches tall, with stick-
like legs and large feet. His chest was buff, with rust-
brown streaks; the feathers on his back were dark brown.
His long tail was propped up unnaturally by a pile of
towels behind him, and his bent-over posture added to
the overall impression of readiness for action. Juvenile
sharp-shinned hawk, I said to myself. Sharpie, as the
slang term went.

Many of the volunteers found sharpies and their
relatives from the accipter family, Cooper's hawks, very
annoying to work with. Unbelievably hyper, with the
reflexes to match, the birds were forever escaping from

people's clutches. We always moved the two species into outside cages as soon as we could. I admired the Ferrari-like acceleration of these bird-hunting sprinters, but I had fallen victim to the frustration they provoked on many occasions. I looked to see how the volunteer was equipped. She wore thin leather gloves for dexterity and held a fine mesh net of the kind seen in tropical-fish stores. Walking quietly to the shelf, I selected a similar net. A larger fish net leaned against the wall, but small raptors could pass easily through its holes. Next I slipped on a pair of lightweight gloves. Focussed on the task at hand, I forgot the habitual heaviness in my limbs. But when the volunteer and I exchanged a smile of camaraderie as we prepared to catch the escapee, my cheeks felt stiff. I realized I hadn't been smiling much lately.

Catching one of the fastest, most manoeuvrable birds in the world takes both luck and excellent hand/eye co-ordination. The volunteer moved towards the young hawk, and as his eyes fastened on her, I moved into a different position, hoping he'd fly in my direction. As always with accipiters, the suddenness of his launch was shocking. I lifted my net by reflex, scooping it over the hawk in the air. I continued the arc and brought him deftly to the ground. Grasping the struggling body, I picked him up, net and all, and looked to the volunteer for direction. She inclined her head towards a freshly cleaned large wooden cage with a bough of Douglas fir tucked into one corner. Its needle-filled branches would provide some camouflage for the nervous bird. Reaching in past the middle of the cage, I placed the net containing the struggling dynamo on the cage's towel-covered floor. Then, in one fast motion, I lifted my hand and the net and lunged backwards. Slamming the cage door, I leaned on it and looked over at the volunteer. "Sharpies!" She expelled her breath forcefully, and we laughed.

Next I moved on to Ichabod's cage. I'd begun to be consistent with particular words and phrases in reference to the eagle's movements. Every time Ichabod moved away from me on her own initiative, for example, I pointed, clucked and said, "Move." Whenever we had an altercation, I used the mop as a shield in addition to the clucking command. Usually she complied, and when she did I threw food down for her. Sometimes, though, nothing I said or did could ward off an attack. When I was in her cage, I always had to keep my wits about me.

Despite these challenges with Ichabod, the dark clouds of depression continued to hang over me. One Saturday morning I lay sprawled across the futon in my small bedroom. My head felt stuffed full of cotton. I looked at my alarm clock: 8:00 A.M., well past the time I needed to get up to be at O.W.L. on time. I lay there for what seemed like a half-hour, but when I looked at the clock again, it was only 8:03. Reluctantly, I roused myself and dressed.

As I breasted the highway overpass in my car, I saw the flats of Mud Bay. A thin skim of silvery water had slipped along a channel in the mud. It looked like a giant crescent, or the rind of some silvery fruit. Though some far-off part of my brain recognized the beauty of the scene, I remained untouched, driving like an automaton along the familiar route. Finally I turned the wheel onto the road leading to O.W.L. The tops of the tall trees lining the road loomed above. A heron flew low overhead, its harsh *kraak, kraak* filling the car as its shadow passed over me. I followed the prehistoric-looking bird in the direction of O.W.L.

I performed the usual rituals once I arrived, greeting volunteers, assigning tasks, checking for new patients and planning the day's medications. Normally I was constantly in motion during my shifts, helping new volunteers to feed the birds, teaching someone how to give an injection. But today, when the office area cleared of people, I stood still, trying to filter out the noise of buckets being filled and cupboards being opened so that I could hear the birds. I wasn't sure exactly what I was listening for, but gradually the quiet shuffling of feathers and the thrum of wings revived me. I set off decisively for the feed room.

"Feeding the 'bod?" a seasoned volunteer asked, using the nickname I secretly detested. I smiled and nodded, suddenly wanting only to be alone with the eagle.

Lifting the mop from the rack, I walked to Ichabod's cage, set the pail down, undid the lock, slipped the eagle glove on my left hand and entered, a dead rat in my bare right hand. The eagle was nowhere in sight. I stood still and listened. I'd left my jacket behind, and I could feel the air moving against the bare skin of my arms.

I heard the whoosh of Ichabod's wings before my eyes registered her presence. She flew over the half wall towards me. The last of my lethargy left me. I stood stock still, mop raised, and waited, aware of the thinness of my polo shirt. This is going to hurt, I thought. The bird seemed to take forever to reach me, and another thought passed through my mind: *suicide by eagle.* Then my body reacted. I lifted the mop in a blur, parrying the thrust of Ichabod's talons, shoving the eagle back. She flapped hard to regain her balance, then attacked again, this time from a slightly different angle. I choked up on the mop and met the thrust of her feet. She hung on, both feet embedded in the mop's locks. The wind from her wings rushed around my head, making me dizzy. Her eyes were two feet from mine. I thrust the mop from me, sliding my hands down the handle. The russet-brown eyes met mine for another instant, then Ichabod released her hold and flew to the half wall. Breathing hard, my hands trembling, I carefully placed the eagle's rat on a nearby stump and backed out of her cage.

I entered the care centre through the back door,

almost running into a pair of volunteers on their way out. "How was Ichabod?" one of them asked. Her voice sounded far away, as if she spoke from the other end of a tunnel.

"Fine," I said. "She was fine."

In the washroom mirror I saw my flushed face, hair in a wild tangle. I leaned on the sink and looked at myself for a long time, as if relearning my own features.

10

FOLLOWING THE FALCONS

THE TALL HAWK left the falconer's glove in a smooth stroke of russet wings. Then, wings fanned out, each long feather articulated clearly against the warm air, the bird landed on the thin branch of a nearby bush, his weight rocking the perch precariously. He bobbed his head to the side, locating the man twenty feet away, before looking farther afield to the small black-and-white dog rooting around in a nest of brambles. The hawk shifted from one foot to the other like a featherweight boxer, then lifted into the air and flew to a thicker willow. Satisfied on the more stable perch, he whisked his tail back and forth and continued to watch both man and dog closely.

I stood near a sandy field in an abandoned gravel pit called Stokes Pit. The abundance of blackberry bushes here provided excellent cover for rabbits. The area's ditches and sloughs were surrounded by trees, and the terrain was in various stages of regrowth. A half-mile away, gravel trucks and other equipment grumbled as stones and sand were hauled out of an active part of the pit. It was a sunny fall day. The hawk's name was Kwah; the man and the dog were Dennis Maynes and his Jack Russell terrier, Daisy. I'd met Dennis through another falconer, Terry Spring.

Today, Dennis wore a green backpack and a jacket of brown and green. Around his neck was a whistle for calling his hawk back to the glove. Swinging his arm rhythmically, Dennis smashed the brambles with a stout branch as the terrier scouted. They were flushing out rabbits for Kwah.

Kwah belonged to a species native to Arizona and New Mexico called Harris hawks. As I stood watching the threesome, a movement in the distance caught my eye. A man was walking across a log that spanned a ditch, his arm held out from his side. As he neared, I could see that he was carrying a hawk, another Harris. These hawks are popular with falconers because they respond quickly to training and also because they are communal hunters in the wild, seeking their prey in groups of up to six birds. For falconers who enjoyed the company of others, the Harris hawk was the perfect bird. Most other species had to be flown alone, since individual birds behaved aggressively towards each other. As the man in the distance drew closer, I could see that his lips were moving. His hawk's head was inclined towards him as if the bird was drinking in every word. I was fascinated by these close relationships between humans and birds. As I turned back to watch Kwah follow Dennis and Daisy on the hunt for rabbits, I envisioned Ichabod flying to my glove, her big wings turning the world dark in the moments before she landed.

A few weeks later, in a blueberry field in Port Coquitlam, I watched falconry of a different sort. The falconer, Terry Spring, stood with a hooded grey gyrfalcon on his left gloved wrist. I noted Terry's every move as he deftly loosened the long leather traces at the back of the hood, taking one trace in his right hand and the other in his teeth. Once he'd loosened the hood enough, he slipped it off the bird's head with his right hand.

Hoods were completely enclosed helmets that allowed no light inside. Each was custom-made of soft leather. Cutting off the vision of a hawk or a falcon allowed the bird to relax, so that it was safe to transport it tethered on a perch in a car rather than confining it to a kennel cab where it could bash around, breaking off feathers and injuring wings. Hooding started at a young age, and most experienced birds, after a brief stroke of the hood against their breast, accepted the head covering with ease.

Terry flew Quest, his falcon, after ducks during duck-hunting season. His huge German wire-haired pointer, Max, would gambol about nearby, nose to the ground. Because falcons hit ducks in midair, crippling or killing them, Quest needed the birds driven off the water before he could take a fair shot at a meal. Max would act as the duck flusher.

As I watched, Terry lifted his backpack off the ground and shoved his hand in, feeling for the pieces of quail he'd use if he needed to call in his falcon. He checked for his whistle where it swung around his neck on a black cord. Bending down while holding his left arm steady in a practised way, he tucked his jeans more securely into his tall rubber boots. Quest shifted on his wrist. Terry looked at the falcon as he straightened up and then made a *chuk, chuk* sound. Quest responded with a similar noise. Lifting his arm high, Terry encouraged the falcon to lift into the air. Quest powered off in a series of rapid flaps, his flight very different from the slow, wide beats of a Harris hawk. The falcon was not honing in on an attractive perch; he meant to stay airborne. Each flap drew him farther from the ground into the world of sky and wind, where he was more at home. Quest's body was small and streamlined, his wings arrow-shaped in flight, his large, long-toed feet pulled back neatly. I imagined the wind breaking over his body, tendrils curling behind like swirls of water behind a boat.

"Max, ducks!" Terry called to the dog. Max galloped

along the dyke. A steep-sided ditch held enough water to satisfy the flotilla of ducks a hundred yards away.

After a minute or two, I wouldn't have known that the small grey shape against the blue was a bird if I hadn't seen Quest fly up there. I pictured the falcon at a thousand feet, cold air nipping his wings, fast-pumping heart flashing blood to his muscles, nerves prompting his warmed muscles to shallow flapping. At times Quest was lost in the brightness, as if swallowed by the sky, and I wondered if Terry was worried. Then the bird would appear again, and I'd feel foolish about my moment of panic. I found out later that falconers too have moments of panic, just not so quickly. Terry told me that all falconers have lost beloved birds.

Terry looked up briefly to check Quest's position. "Waiting on" is the term for a falcon holding position over the falconer and dog or the prospective prey. I knew that once the prey was flushed, Quest would drop head first, or "stoop," at a speed of about two hundred miles an hour.

Terry turned his attention to the ducks as Max got closer to them. When the dog crossed some invisible line of safety, the ducks splashed to the air. My head snapped up to watch for the falcon, but even then I almost missed him, such was his speed as he dropped through the air. The ducks sprinted to their full speed, which can be close to forty-five miles an hour, but one bird veered off alone. The falcon aimed towards this one. In an instant, he hit the duck with a loud crack. Feathers burst into the air as if from a ripped pillow. The duck fell like a stone to the grass. The falcon pulled from his dive, arching upwards momentarily, before dropping back down to his fallen prey.

Terry approached his bird quietly as the falcon started plucking feathers from the duck. Reaching into his back-pack, he pulled out a piece of quail. He crouched and extended his gloved hand, quail meat held firmly in it, to Quest. "Up! Up!" he said softly. Quest dithered for a moment but then stepped onto the glove and returned to Terry. While the falcon fed on the quail, Terry stood and shoved the duck behind him with his foot, removing it from the falcon's sight. Duck would be on Terry's dinner plate tonight, and he'd share the remains with Quest later.

The skills and equipment used by falconers like Terry and Dennis originated long ago. This form of co-operative hunting was done in China and the Middle East. One Middle Eastern bas-relief of a falconer with his hawk is dated at 750 B.C. By the third or fourth century A.D. falconry was common in central Europe, though it would be several more centuries before it appeared in Britain. Once it did, the sport gained popularity fast. Certain birds were reserved for use by British royalty; the peregrine falcon was reserved for the king. Kestrels were ladies' birds, and the general population made use of the versatile goshawk. Raptors began to appear on coats of arms and family crests. Birds of prey were used to hunt food for the table, and over time hunting dogs were developed to flush and find game for hawks and falcons. The hoods, jesses and leashes shown in old drawings bear a remarkable resemblance to the modern falconer's equipment. The knots to fasten jesses around a bird's leg or to tie a falcon to a perch also have their origins in ancient times. Shakespeare used falconry terms such as "stoop," "lure" and "bate" with obvious familiarity. But with the increased use of guns as well as the loss of forest to farmland, interest in falconry waned.

Today, a relatively small number of people practise the sport, though many regions have clubs. The North American Falconry Association holds a giant meet every year that is well attended by falconers from Canada and the United States. Falconry catalogues sell everything from books, gloves and leashes to perches and traps for capturing wild raptors.

I'd seen Terry and Quest give demonstrations at schools and environmental clubs. At those times, Terry would use a ducklike leather lure to call the falcon down. Children always looked delighted as the falcon stooped on the lure. Afterwards Terry would stand casually, the bird on his glove, answering questions. Occasionally there'd be a lull, and Terry would turn to Quest, *chuk, chuk*ing as if asking the falcon a question. Quest would respond in kind, arousing more delight in the audience.

Spending time out in the fields with falconers and their birds made me long for the country. Later that fall, I heard of an opportunity that combined accommodation on a farm with a part-time job. The job involved working for the University of British Columbia, taking care of a number of small, quail-like birds called tinamous. The man who owned the farm leased part of the property to the university. I made arrangements to meet the supervisor.

My first sight of the farm enthralled me. It looked like a Spanish garrison, all made of stone. A tower rose in the far corner, and a windmill turned lazily. Perched high on the tower was a peacock shrilling its eerie cry. As I entered a small courtyard, guinea fowl ran under my feet. Old horse stalls fitted with wooden doors ringed the courtyard, and in the corner farthest from the tower was an apartment I figured must have been the stable manager's quarters at one time. This was the accommodation that came with the job. The old stalls held tinamous now, and out behind the stone house was an aviary that housed various species of waterfowl.

The job entailed feeding and caring for the tinamous and then collecting their shiny, chocolate-brown eggs, putting them into an incubator to hatch. Hoping it wouldn't jeopardize my chance at the job, I mentioned to the supervisor that I volunteered at O.W. L. on Saturdays. He was fine with that, and he hired me on the spot.

The Nicomekl River wound its way past the property, and as I walked back to my car, I could make out parts

of a yacht bobbing in the water. The traffic on the highway in the distance sounded like faint rushing water. I
watched a female harrier quarter the field beside the
driveway. She was a good omen, I figured.

I moved to my new home a few weeks later, leaving
the concrete and the bustle of the city behind. Though
I was unused to living where employers might knock
on my door and ask chores of me at any time, I felt
good about my space and was interested in soaking
up new skills. The horses I rode were farther away now,
but I drove to the stables several times a week to ride
for anyone who had a horse needing exercise. I'd also
developed a relationship with an instructor that allowed
me to do spare work for her in exchange for lessons.
I used any excuse to place my hands on the satiny skin
of horses. Being able to lean against the big bodies,
breathing in their scent and throwing my arm over their
wide backs, reminded me what an accessible feast for the
senses horses were. That was in striking contrast to the
raptors I had to drink in from afar.

I had continued to work with Ichabod on the glove.
She was three and a half now, and I stood eye to eye
with her with little difficulty when she had her big feet
wrapped around my gloved arm. When I extended my
arm beside me at waist height, her shoulders were level
with mine; in that position, in fact, every part of her,
from chest upwards, lined up with the parts of my body.

But touching her as a way of making contact was out of the question. I would sometimes tent my fingers over her keel to check her weight, but this was done only when she was relaxed after a feeding or distracted. Although she sometimes seemed to accept this touch grudgingly, I never fooled myself into thinking that she liked it.

Ichabod's blocky beak was starting to shade lighter, towards the yellow it would become. Her head had a mottled appearance now, the brown no longer predominant. The bony protuberance over her eyes shaded them forbiddingly, but even with that I could see they had lightened to a ginger colour.

One afternoon Ichabod and I stood quietly in her cage. The scritching of her talons against my glove was the only sound. I rested my left arm on the branch behind us for stability. As I slumped a little, Ichabod did the same, pulling her neck into her body and hunching her shoulders. It made her look like a vulture. I smiled at the sight. "You don't look so regal now," I said aloud. She turned her head at my words and looked me squarely in the eye before turning back to gaze across the field.

After a minute her beak opened, and a small noise came out. "What was that?" I asked. As if in answer, she repeated the noise, more loudly this time. It sounded a bit like the croaking of a frog. She continued to look out across the field, croaking, until her eyes lit on something of interest. The croaking stopped abruptly. I strained to see what she was looking at, but the field seemed empty. Then I caught a glimpse of movement on the far-off dyke. A dog running. Ichabod flexed and released her talons on the scarred leather of my glove. She began to make noises again, this time with greater variety. She croaked, chortled and cawed. "Blabbermouth," I said to her, delighted with this new behaviour. She threw me another glance and simultaneously tightened her grip on my arm. "Ow," I said in response. She turned back to the field, and gradually her grip lightened in intensity, until her toes and talons were draped loosely around the wrist and forearm of my gloved arm. Her posture stiffened again as an eagle flew across the dyke far in the distance. Sightseeing with an eagle, I thought.

A commotion outside the cage roused both of us. A clatter of buckets signified volunteers returning from feeding the birds in the nearby cages. Lifting my arm slowly and carefully, I pivoted until the eagle and I were facing a perch. "Off!" I said. Ichabod looked at me and gripped the glove in answer. I repeated, "Off!" The eagle grew tall and dropped her wings from her shoulders. For a moment I thought excitedly, she's going! Then she gripped the glove hard again and settled her wings around her body fussily, as if to say "No!"

I'd discovered an unusual problem while working Ichabod on the glove. Using Terry's command of "Up! Up!" to ask her to step onto the glove usually worked, but getting her off was a different story. The falconers I'd asked about this found it strange. For some reason, she didn't want to let go of the glove.

This time, I spontaneously reached into my pocket for a pinkie. Ichabod's head snapped my way, her expression intent. Stepping closer to the half wall, I slapped the pinkie down quickly and said, "Off!" The eagle catapulted from the glove, smacking me in the head with one of her wings, and landed on the pinkie, squashing it flat. Scraping it from the wood, she swallowed the morsel avidly. I was out the door before she could look for more. Well, that works, I thought. I had something new to add to my repertoire.

LATER THAT DAY, one of O.W.L.'s directors told me formally that, since no one else could deal with Ichabod, she didn't see a place for the eagle at the care centre. I searched the woman's face and saw only an implacable firmness. When I realized this was no ordinary conversation, my stomach did a flip. After that, I heard the director's voice as if from far away. My mind raced through various options as she talked. It seemed unlikely that the provincial government branch that dealt with raptor permits would grant an individual a permit for an eagle. In any case, I couldn't grasp the thought of moving Ichabod; the logistics seemed insurmountable. Silently, I disputed the fact that the eagle would never be useful for educational purposes. As I tried to picture my life without Ichabod, panic cramped my gut.

I tuned back in just as the director was saying that someone could get hurt dealing with such a bird. I could see where she was going now. I knew zoos wouldn't take Ichabod. Bald eagles were relatively common, and I remembered how O.W.L. had searched unsuccessfully for a zoo placement for a non-releasable adult male eagle a few years back. Clearly, the director was leading up to euthanasia as the only option.

Resolve straightened my spine. On the bulletin board behind the director, I could see a sheet of paper listing the names and phone numbers of the other O.W.L. directors. I wasn't sure when the next monthly meeting was, but I made up my mind to call the other directors before that meeting with a plan. What the plan would be, however, I didn't know yet. Desperate now to get away from the scene, I made some noncommittal noises and then escaped. As I walked to the back of the care centre, my face felt tight with anxiety. Although the news had not come as a complete surprise, I was still shocked by the suddenness of it.

As I drove home that afternoon, I thought of various ways I could train Ichabod to take part in O.W.L.'s educational program. Perhaps I could use falconry methods with her, putting on displays for groups of people who were kept back a safe distance with a barrier. That evening, I spent hours on the telephone, pitching my idea to board members. I argued that Ichabod deserved a chance and made clear that I was willing to commit to her. Each time I put the phone down, my insides clenched with fear. Could I possibly get the entire board of directors to agree to my plan? Even if they did, would I be able to carry out the necessary training with so much at stake? But each time, I reassured myself I could do it.

That night I dreamed I stood in a field with my arm outstretched, waiting for Ichabod to land on the glove. As the moments passed my arm grew weary, but I forced myself to hold it out from my side. My arm began to throb. Suddenly I felt the shock of Ichabod's grasp on my forearm and smiled with relief. But when I turned to look at her, there was no eagle there, only my trembling gloved arm stretching so far away from me it looked tiny.

In the morning, I drafted a letter to Fish and Wildlife, the branch of the provincial government in charge of issuing permits to both rehabilitation centres and falconers. The branch would already know of Ichabod, since O.W.L. had to report all non-releasable birds to their office. Not wanting to take any chances, I decided to deliver my proposal in person. At the branch office, I found two conservation officers who were willing to talk to me.

Nervously, I outlined my plan. Since I already knew that eagles flown by falconers could not fly free in populated areas, I told the biologists I would train Ichabod to fly to my glove outside her cage using a long, light-weight line falconers called a creance. The public could view our demonstrations from a position safely out of range. The officers gave me a verbal okay, though they said they would need to study my proposal further. For now, I would be able to report to O.W.L.'s board that

Fish and Wildlife had given me tentative permission.

At their meeting later that month, the board of directors decided to give me six months to prove that Ichabod was trainable. I was elated: the first part of my plan had worked. Now all I had to do was follow through on the rest. It was a daunting challenge, but one I was determined to meet.

11

CUSTOM-MADE

WORKING AT THE research aviary paid my rent but left little for gas and food. Because I had to feed the birds there as well as tend to the eggs in the incubators, it was difficult to find other part-time work. And my supervisor at the aviary was starting to pressure me to work there on weekends rather than going to O.W.L. The situation worried me, since once I started Ichabod's formal training, I would need to go to O.W.L. during the week as well. My plan was to visit O.W.L. in the early mornings, then return to my work at the aviary. Reluctantly, I had decided to put horses on the back burner for the time being.

I read as much as I could about falconry, and I thought about it nonstop. I called all the falconers I knew to talk about my work with Ichabod, but what they told me was not encouraging. First of all, though falconers worked regularly with golden eagles, bald eagles were not seen as traditional falconry birds. There were several examples of bird trainers in the U.S. being badly injured by "balds," and bald eagles were considered less stable in temperament than goldens due to their aggressive, squabbling nature in the wild. Secondly, Ichabod was three and a half years old, with little formal training. Third, she was an imprint. This, combined with her natural aggression, would make it very dangerous to work with her using food as a motivator.

In falconry training, a bird receives food only from the falconer, which can make dinnertime a high-stakes power game. Although aggression sometimes comes out in imprinted falcons, many falconers raise their birds in such a way as to avoid imprinting them to people. And a falcon being aggressive is, as one falconer put it, "a whole different kettle of fish from a huge eagle being aggressive!" When I explained that I had already used food as a motivator with Ichabod, the reply was invariably a laugh and some version of "You ain't seen nothin' yet." Each time I responded stubbornly that I still wanted to give it a try. The falconers I talked to supported that, and several offered their help.

I started to attend falconry gatherings whenever I could, and before long I found myself picking up the lingo. The term "passage bird" denotes a wild-caught adult hawk or falcon. "Tercel" means a male falcon, while the word "falcon" is used to indicate the female bird. The word "eyas" is used for a hawk or falcon of any age that was taken as a youngster from the nest; "haggard" is a hawk or falcon captured after it has its mature plumage. My head was filled with terms such as "cadge," a portable perch used to carry one or more (usually hooded) hawks or falcons in the field, and "yarak," the state of readiness to kill that shows itself in particular postures of a raptor. Watching Dennis Maynes calm an excitable red-tail and another falconry club member, Trevor Mellish, placate his merlin, I realized that the techniques they used came from centuries of research into the safe handling of birds of prey.

The methodology of falconry is simply reward-based training. To begin with, food is held in the falconer's gloved hand, and the raptor has to step onto the glove to get it. Gradually the falconer will stand farther back from the perch, asking the bird to cover more distance, and the bird will "hop" or "bounce" to the glove. All along, the glove is associated with food. After a while the bird will step willingly onto the glove even when no food is present, since it knows that at some point it will be fed.

I stood in Dennis's back yard one afternoon, watching him prepare his Harris hawk to go out hunting. I paid close attention to the details of what he did. Which part of the glove did he prefer the bird to stand on? How did he hold the jesses fastened around the bird's legs? Jesses, swivels, falconer's knots, creance lines: it was a whole new world of equipment and skills. Most of the equipment was fastened and unfastened with the falconer's right hand, because the bird stood on his gloved left hand. Left-handed falconers worked in the opposite way.

I had some dexterity with this kind of equipment from working with Lucy, the educational red-tailed hawk at O.W.L. She wore jesses and a leather leash that split at the end into two pieces, each with its own snap, somewhat like the leashes people use to walk two dogs at once. The split pieces were threaded through slits in the bottom of the jesses. But what kind of equipment would work with an eagle, I wondered. Most of what I'd seen was not suited to an eagle's size or strength. Finally, through a falconry catalogue, I ordered a leather leash and some jesses customized to Ichabod's species and weight.

While I was waiting for the equipment to arrive, I scouted out the cage that was to be Ichabod's new home. The falconers I'd spoken to were unanimous in saying that, if I wanted to start a new training regime with the eagle, it would be easier to do that in a new territory. O.W.L. had a three-hundred-foot flight cage that was divided into sections by giant sliding doors. The cage was designed to allow the structure either to become one cage, when the sliding doors were open, or to be sectioned off into six separate cages, with the sliding doors closed and locked. The last section, closed off, would be Ichabod's new cage. It was located at the very back of the property, so the young eagle would be able to observe the other O.W.L. cages across the field as well as the comings and goings of volunteers. The wall facing the field had wood coming up to a height of four feet from the ground, then chain-link reaching to twelve feet above. The chain-link continued as the roof for another fifteen feet, until a wood roof took over. The wall along the back of the cage was solid, as was the cage door.

As I looked out through the chain-link, I saw a red-winged blackbird grasp a twig close to the cage; the bird opened its throat and let out a loud, sharp *check,* then released a longer, noted call. I could hear splashing in the pond hidden behind brambles on the cage's east side. After a minute, two mallards accelerated over the top of the brambles and flew south towards Boundary Bay.

I liked the view from here, and I hoped Ichabod would too. Behind me a notched log stood on end. It would make a good strut for a perch, I thought. In the sheltered area of the cage, a platform stood six feet above the ground. I decided to put several good perching logs on the platform, but no perches near the door. If I could predict where Ichabod was coming from, I'd have a better chance of staying safe.

Ichabod remained in her old cage while I readied the new one. As I unlocked the door to her old cage one morning, I ran through a checklist in my head. Glove—check. Mop—check. I had decided to continue taking the mop along, though no falconer would be caught dead with such a thing. I patted the chest pocket of my jacket for rat pieces. I was trying to feed Ichabod mostly on the glove, but since I was still coming into O.W. L. only on the weekends, food was thrown into her cage on the days I was away.

As I opened the cage door, I saw Ichabod come to attention on her outside perch. She opened her wings and hopscotched from the perch to the half wall. Her legs swung forward as she landed, settling her wings neatly around herself.

I approached, pulling the glove onto my left hand and arm. Ichabod chirred softly, her friendly call. When I was about two feet from her, I turned my back. As my right hand felt for a piece of rat in my chest pocket, I watched her over my shoulder. Stretching out my left arm, I quickly placed the rat between my leather-clad thumb and index finger, then closed my hand around it. Still looking over my shoulder, I gave the usual command: "Up! Up!"

Ichabod reached out with one half-open foot towards the food. I moved another step away from the half wall. She withdrew her foot, holding it in the air for a minute in a fastidious manner, then setting it down and raising the other one. She's not hungry, I thought; that's what a falconer would say. Ichabod moved her raised foot towards my arm again. When she couldn't quite reach it, she withdrew her foot, chattering uncertainly.

I tightened my fingers around the rat piece and repeated, "Up! Up!"

The eagle straightened, and I could see certainty shoot through her body like an electric current. She jumped and landed hard, rocking my arm. The foot farthest from me, her left foot, covered the food completely. Her right foot had landed where the glove met my bunched-up jacket at the elbow.

I raised my gloved hand higher than my shoulder, inviting the bird to move to the highest point. Ichabod opened her wings and beat them twice, the closest wing brushing my head. Even with her body at this crazy angle, she hung on stubbornly. My manoeuvre was a risky one: in this position, the eagle's head was much closer to my face. Just as I had decided to lower my arm, Ichabod lifted her right foot from my jacket and shifted herself to a narrower stance. I breathed a sigh of relief.

The eagle opened her left foot and reached to pull the piece of rat through my glove. I let her reveal some more of the piece but held firmly to the rest. She settled her body over the food, one talon from each foot dug into the rat's exposed flesh to brace it. Then her beak swept down and hooked onto the meat, ripping off a strip. After demolishing the exposed part, she reached down to pull more of the rat piece into view. I gradually released the remaining morsel until the eagle was finished. She looked expectantly towards me. Time for her to jump off the glove, then ask her back on for another piece. I turned around so that we were facing the half wall. "Off!" I said.

154

Ichabod looked at the wall, jerked slightly, then settled back on the glove. I repeated the command, swinging my arm slightly towards the wall. She gripped my moving arm harder. My arm was getting tired. I tried again. "Off!" Ichabod glanced at the wall, then back at me, her eyes resting on my face.

Suddenly, her talons clenched hard to my glove. I couldn't believe the pressure. It was as if, up to this point in our work, Ichabod had just been playing with me. One talon pressed hard into the base of my gloved thumb. Numbness travelled up my arm. I rolled my wrist, hoping to force the bird to loosen her grip. Again I had a picture of Ichabod climbing the glove towards my face. Sweat trickled down my sides. Stupid, stupid, I chided myself, to try this without jesses. I tamped down the panic in my stomach, hoping the eagle hadn't sensed the brief upsurge. I drew a deep breath and took stock. The odds were good that if I put food on the half wall, the eagle would get off the glove. If I timed the placement of the food with the word command, then she'd get a reward for complying. At least that way I'd salvage some control over the situation, I thought ruefully.

The trick would be to get the remaining piece of food out of my pocket. I cursed myself for the size of it. It was the upper portion of a large rat, and I could see now that I should have cut it into smaller pieces. But it was too late for that. As I slipped my free hand into my pocket as unobtrusively as possible, I couldn't help picturing Ichabod releasing my arm to go straight for the food. She turned her head towards me. I held my breath, remaining still for a heartbeat. Then she lifted her head towards some sight in the distance. I released my breath slowly.

I fumbled in my increasingly gooey pocket until I found the head of the rat. If I could brace the rat's chest against something, I could probably pull off its head. A voice in my head chastised me: C'mon, just put the whole piece on the wall and be done with it! But the stubborn side of me won out. I shifted towards the half wall, trying to keep my gloved arm still. I was rewarded with the tightened clench of a talon on my thumb. Bending my knees, I pushed my pocket against the wall and pulled hard on the rat's head. My left arm trembled with the effort of keeping steady, but the eagle stayed quiet. The head came loose, and I concealed it in my right hand. I gritted my teeth and stepped back from the wall. The accompanying crush of talons made me gasp.

My left thumb hurt bone-deep, although I knew the talon had not pierced the leather.

I drew my right hand forward. Ichabod's head swivelled, tracking the movement. I dropped the rat's head on the half wall. The word "Off!" had barely left my lips when the eagle leapt from my glove to pounce squarely on the rat piece. Ichabod turned her head sideways and chirred playfully while I rubbed my dented thumb. Then, picking up the rat's head in her beak, she swallowed it whole. I backed out of the cage as she was eating, pushing away the image of my own head clenched in the feet that now sat so benignly on the edge of the half wall.

THE FALCONERS I'd met locally corresponded with falconers around the world, and sometimes falconers from other countries would arrive for a visit. I met a South African and a German falconer at a get-together at Dennis Maynes's house. Their visit coincided with the arrival of the falconry equipment I'd ordered. Both visitors, experienced with golden eagles, vetoed the leash and the precut jesses the minute they saw them. The leather wouldn't be strong enough, they said. The German man explained that leash and jess leather should not give or stretch at all when you pulled on it. They suggested that I buy a much stronger piece of leather for the jesses and use rock-climbing rope for both the leash and the long creance I'd use to fly Ichabod. According to the foreign falconers, carabiners, lightweight metal clips with spring latches used in climbing, would be the best tools for attaching the jesses to the leash or the creance.

As it turned out, Thys Wallace, the South African falconer, was in B.C. on an extended visit, and he had been invited to work with a large female bald eagle from a nearby game farm. A movie being shot locally required a bald eagle. The training had already started by the time I heard about it, but I was anxious to witness the work he was doing with the bird.

The first time I saw Esther, the game-farm eagle, she was perched in the back of a windowless van. A heavy canvas curtain separated her from the driver. The bird's jesses were attached to a leash pulled through a ring set in the perch's heavy base. Because Esther's training had not started until she was an adult, she was difficult to hood successfully. The canvas and the windowless back of the van kept her calm while travelling.

I watched the eagle's snowy-white crest rise as Thys offered her his glove. She was reluctant to leave the perch at first, but after a long pause she stepped onto the glove. With his free hand, Thys unhooked her leash and fastened it to a ring on his belt.

The falconer lifted the bird clear of the van in one smooth motion. Esther's head snaked towards Thys's face, and he grinned as he kept his face out of range, holding the eagle well away from his body. Moments later, she· tried again. Thys stayed relaxed through all of this.

I heard someone behind me say that since the bird had came late to training, naturally she would be difficult to work with. I mulled this over, thinking of Ichabod.

Despite Esther's attempts at face-biting, she was co-operative, if grudgingly so. Yet she remained in her own world, gazing haughtily into the distance with the classic look of the eagles. Esther was a mature adult eagle imprinted to her own kind. Thus her lunges at the falconer's face were half-hearted, exhibiting none of the particular aggression towards humans that Ichabod's actions carried.

A few days later I headed downtown to a store that specialized in mountaineering gear. As I drove towards the tunnel that led under the Fraser River, I glanced over at a dead snag by the water's edge. I knew eagles sometimes perched there, as well as on the nearby live trees with their well-spaced boughs. I checked the rearview mirror, then slowed down as much as I could get away with to prolong my ability to see the river. I scanned the trees and the horizon. Just as my car dipped down on the approach to the tunnel, I made out the dark form of a juvenile eagle sitting high in a tree. "That's number six," I said aloud. It was a game I played with myself, counting the number of birds of prey I could spot from the road. I was always thrilled when I caught sight of fast, nervy hawks such as the sharp-shinned or Cooper's. On my last trip into the concrete jungle, I'd seen a Cooper's hawk flash across the road carrying a robin. Peering up from behind the steering wheel to identify hawks made for some sporadic driving, though, and I'd have to stop looking whenever I encountered heavy traffic.

All along the walls of the mountaineering store hung large spools of thin nylon rope in primary colours. Carabiners glinted in glass cabinets, and I noticed one lying on the counter. As a staffperson and a young man in a green bandanna exchanged stories about climbing some-thing they called the Chief, I fingered the smooth metal of the carabiner, then rolled the locking device down-wards; that freed the bottom lip to press inward under pressure. I mimed sliding it through the narrow slits in the eagle's jesses. I rolled the locking mechanism back up and tested to see that the oblong shape of the carabiner stayed rigid, trapping the imaginary jesses in its grasp. I opened and closed the carabiner several more times, en-joying the neat, satisfying click of its metal parts.

I bought a carabiner and a rolled-up length of bright purple climbing rope, then set out for my next stop, a leather store. I walked out of there carrying a bundle of thin, strong leather of the sort the salesclerk told me was used to keep boats from chafing against the wood of a dock.

Once I got home, I cut strips twelve inches long and one inch wide from the leather and then softened them with a conditioner. The leather glowed as I laid it out across a small board. The strips seemed long compared to the jesses I'd seen on hawks, but the falconers had said that I'd appreciate the length when I was working with the eagle.

The making of the actual jesses would involve cutting slits in a precise place on each of these strips, so that when one end of the leather was pulled through the slit it would make a perfect anklet for the eagle, neither too loose nor too snug. Tiny cuts along the edge of the leather would allow the anklets to curl gently around the bird's legs. I'd leave this work to the falconers until I became more practised at it.

That night I dreamed of scanning the sky for birds. A thin layer of clear air wrapped like a glove over the land, cushioning me against space. I waved my hand back and forth through it.

I woke disoriented. Realizing it wasn't morning yet, I lay awake thinking about air. The Inuit have words for many different kinds of snow. Were there people somewhere who worshipped the mythological creatures that traversed the sky, as well as those alive and breathing? Did those people have many words for air?

12

JESSING AN EAGLE

THE DYKE by the Nicomekl River curved through the farmland along the river's path, matching it in a sinuous wind. Like the spine of a dormant sea serpent, the dyke uncoiled under my feet. Swallows skated through the cool air, scooping insects inches from the water's surface.

My continued refusal to miss weekend shifts at O.W.L. had become a constant source of tension between me and my employers at the aviary. I clashed with my supervisor more often than not. I had also discovered that living where I worked was not conducive to the privacy I needed.

Today I'd been given one month's notice to vacate the corner apartment. *Fired.* I mouthed the word to myself, trying it on for size. I was ashamed, yet relieved. My work with Ichabod would no longer be jeopardized.

Determined to stay in a country setting, I looked through the local papers that afternoon for rental accommodation on an acreage. A horse farm in Cloverdale caught my eye, and an hour later I was driving through an open gate in my dilapidated brown Malibu—my "new" car after the old grey boat had packed it in. The Malibu was full of stuff: clothes, boots, books, candy wrappers and even an old lampshade. As I unfolded from the driver's seat, I hoped my prospective landlord wouldn't notice the clutter.

This farm wasn't close to water. The rising and falling of the tides wouldn't affect my phone line here, I thought with a tinge of sadness, as it had at the Nicomekl address. But I liked what I could see of the huge grey barn, grey wood fences and cheerful little blue house. The sheds in each horse field were painted the same shade.

Over tea, the gracious landlady and I spoke of our kindred fascination with horses. Before we knew it, an hour had passed. She had one room available for rent, and the rest of the house would be shared. I decided to take it. The room I'd be in was cozy, with large windows facing the horse fields.

As I walked to the car, a flash of feathers startled me. Though there was no longer any sign of it, I knew in my bones that a sharp-shinned hawk had skimmed over my head. A great blue heron, neck folded neatly into its body, flew with huge wing beats down the road ahead of me as I drove away.

IT WAS TIME to move Ichabod to her new cage. The move went smoothly, and a few days afterwards, the foreign falconers came to fit the eagle with soft leather jesses.

We had decided that it would be easier and safer for the men to net Ichabod rather than try to snatch her off my gloved arm. Nonetheless, I was not looking forward to the ordeal. I stood outside the cage as the men entered. I kept the door slightly ajar, since the new cage had no window set in the door. My stomach twisted as I glimpsed Ichabod's fear. She made herself tall and rangy, head craned high and wings half opened, as she stared at the men. She flapped her wings, then lifted off from her perch, careening past the men straight for the tiny crack in the door—and my face. Shocked, I slammed the door, and she crashed into the wood moments later. I expected more flapping, but I heard nothing. I cracked the door open again. The German falconer, Reiner, already had the net around Ichabod. Thys worked at untangling her.

Once the eagle was extricated, Reiner held her, wings tightly bound, in his arms. Turning so that Ichabod faced away from the door, he sat down on a stump.

As previously planned, I slipped into the cage with an eagle hood in my hand. Grasping Ichabod's head from behind, I slipped her beak through the hole and slid the hood back over her eyes. I didn't realize how much tension she'd been holding in her body until I saw it leak from her like a tire losing air.

I left the cage briefly to get the jesses. As we prepared to fit them, the three of us worked silently to reduce the stress to the eagle. Thys held the straps around Ichabod's lower legs and marked a spot on each piece of leather with a scalpel. Stretching the leather tight across a flat piece of wood, he cut slits in the places he'd marked. Near each end, both leather straps already had two slits cut an inch and a half apart. Thys curled one leather strap around Ichabod's leg above her foot, pulling the end of the strap through one of the slits he'd cut. Slipping the same end through the second of the slits, he fastened the jess securely to Ichabod's ankle, leaving the bight—the rest of the leather strap—hanging free, ready to be grasped. After fastening a jess around the eagle's other leg, Thys cut slits in the bights of both jesses so there would be something to snap a leash onto. He tested the size of the anklets by rotating them back and forth, making sure each moved on Ichabod's ankle, or tarsus.

The men nodded at each other. Thys stood back as Reiner stood up, still holding Ichabod. I reached forward and loosened the straps at the back of the hood. As I backed out of the cage, Thys slipped Ichabod's hood off and Reiner set the eagle on the stump. The falconers followed me out of the cage door. Mission accomplished.

A FEW DAYS later, Thys returned for a training session with Ichabod. I looked in through the chain-link as he entered the cage. Ichabod stood as if dazed, then flew to the stump on her platform. She started to worry the leather on her legs with her beak. I wondered how long the jesses would stand up to her attempts to get rid of them.

Because Ichabod was so disoriented, she was willing to accept others in her new territory. When Thys offered her the glove, she willingly stepped on. He spoke to her in his soft, accented voice, holding the eagle aloft with reverence. I'd seen him treat his captive-bred gyrfalcon, purchased from a local breeder, with the same deference. From watching him, I'd already learned many subtleties of handling raptors.

Thys stood with his arm held out casually. Ichabod grasped his glove lightly with her big feet. Her shoulders were dropped and her wings hung low, as if preparing to flap. I guessed she was getting ready to leave the glove. Thys watched her calmly. The eagle dropped her wings still further and crouched. Then she straightened, settling her wings about her as if shrugging a sweater over her shoulders. Her eyes focussed on something in the distance, and I wondered if she'd caught a glimpse of a volunteer moving through another cage. Thys was humming, and Ichabod turned back to him. With barely a dropped wing in warning, she leapt off the glove in a thunderous crash of feathers. The jesses brought her up short, and she swung below Thys's glove.

When Lucy leapt from the glove, or bated, she usually hung under the glove by her jesses momentarily, then righted herself by flying back up to the glove. If I had mistakenly allowed too much length in the jesses or did not hold tightly to the length I had, Lucy would swing in a wider arc under the glove and was apt to bash a wing on a nearby object.

Hanging below Thys's glove, Ichabod made whimpering sounds. She still swung slightly from the momentum of her leap, like a pendulum coming to rest. "This is what you do, just like this," Thys said to me as he swooped his right hand down to the eagle's outer thigh and, with a light push, swung the eagle behind his left arm. She opened her wings instantly and continued the arc, flying up onto the glove. The whole movement had a continuous grace, man and bird working together. Moments later, Ichabod bated again, leaping to fly, then stopping short at the end of the jesses and nose-diving towards the ground. Moving with the same theatrical flourish, Thys seemed barely to touch the eagle's thigh before she was back on the glove again.

Thys continued his visits to O.W.L., and I enjoyed

watching the young eagle with the expert falconer. But I knew Ichabod would increase her aggression as she became territorial in the new cage. One afternoon, with the apprehension of a student soon to be left to her own devices, I found myself wishing Thys lived in B.C. Then I thought of Terry and Dennis and the other helpful local falconers, and I relaxed. I moved my eyes from Thys's long-boned face to the eagle's. For a moment, the two of them looked curiously similar.

Several days later, I prepared to enter Ichabod's cage on my own for the first time. I hadn't found a new job yet, and my mind jumped back and forth between worry about my finances and the mundane matter of whether I should feed the eagle rats or muskrats. I knew that Ichabod loved muskrat, but the skinned pieces were hard to hold in my gloved hand. For today, I put two small rats in the bottom of my white bucket.

My mind shifted back to my precarious financial state. I'd been trying to find work for several months now with no luck. I drove my car as little as possible to save money, but, living on the farm, I couldn't completely do without a vehicle. I liked my room in the little blue house, especially my view of the horses grazing in the fields. I needed the privacy and open spaces of the country like a drug. Every time I thought of moving to a residential area on a bus route, as my parents had suggested, my face tightened into a mask that made smiling feel foreign.

Rounding the corner of the cages at the back of the care centre, I felt the wind feather my face as if it were something alive, drawing my attention away from my worries. I could sense the potential of the dark rain clouds even before I saw them layered on the horizon. I automatically turned back for a rain jacket, then stopped. I liked the building anticipation of rain on my skin. I looked out along the long row of cages. A hundred feet away, in the nearest cage of the joined sections, a pair of eagles stood high on their perches, white heads thrown back. I had a strong desire to skip ahead and seek out the last occupant in the row. But I curbed my impatience and made myself study each cage. Looking at the other birds relaxed me, and I'd discovered that even in her old cage this relaxation had improved my chances of a peaceful encounter with Ichabod. Sometimes I could see only a wing moving here and there in a cage. Sometimes the whole bird stood in plain view, like the grey great horned owl.

I knew Ichabod could see me from where I was. What kind of behaviour would she exhibit now that she could watch me approach through the field? In her previous cages, there was only the sudden appearance of a face in the window and the sound of a lock drawn through the hasp to alert her that someone intended to enter her domain.

For the past three years, Ichabod and I had existed in our own little realm. But everything had been reshaped by the presence of the falconers. Now someone else had entered the nimbus of power around her, felt the aura she gave off when standing on the glove. I didn't miss the exclusivity, but I wanted my connection with the bird to remain unchanged. Everything was shifting under my feet, and the uncertainty worried me. Although I hadn't spoken about it to anyone, I recognized that Ichabod had become therapy for me. She grounded me in an elemental world where touching a particular perch was an insult, where a hose was a green snake, where a moving black speck on the horizon transfixed the watcher to the exclusion of all else. Outside problems seldom retained a hold on me in the presence of the eagle.

By the time my eyes settled on the last section in the giant flight cage, I was hungry for the sight of Ichabod. From where I stood, I could make out the lone figure of the eagle standing on the perch set into the notched log. I wished there was a way to spy on her, to watch her moods and actions without my presence distracting her. Was she antsy in this cool, rainy weather? Did she stand on the perch near the chain-link at night, or retreat to the platform?

I started down the row with my eyes locked on her. My presence caused rustling and brief flights in the cages I passed, so I moved out as far across the field as possible to avoid disturbing those birds. From there, I could see the eagle at the end much more clearly.

All of a sudden Ichabod shrieked, unfolded her wings and flapped hard twice. She levitated above the perch, then landed again lightly, poised as if touching down for only a moment. I swung the bucket against my leg as I angled towards her cage, and her eyes rested on it as I drew closer.

Ichabod's perch, with one end fitted into the notched log and the other nailed to the low wooden wall, allowed her to stand very close to the chain-link. I was just inches from her now. Her feet were at waist height; her face was at the same height as mine. She inclined her head sideways and made a chirring sound.

As I walked through the narrow corridor between the huge nest of brambles stretching over my head and the high wooden end of the cage, I could hear ducks splashing in the pond behind the brambles. A ring-necked pheasant squawked hoarsely. By some trick of acoustics, these sounds seemed especially loud and clear, as did those coming from inside the cage. Ichabod's feathers crackled like bunched-up paper. I heard the groan of the perch, then the harsh crack of wings as she took off. She landed again: on the log on the corner platform, I guessed. The tower of Boundary Bay Airport loomed behind me as I rounded the corner to the cage door. I looked down the long row of identical doors to my right. Three hundred feet. Thirty horse strides, I thought. I often imagined distances as if I was riding them.

I couldn't pass an open field without thinking about what it would be like to gallop over it. And since moving to the farm, I received my "horse fix" right at home. Late in the evening I could stand in the barn in my nightgown and listen to horse sounds: the soft sighs and shuffling, the rhythmic quiet munching. I drank in the scent of horses through the open window of my bedroom, and the horses in the pasture beside the house peered in at me.

After fitting the small silver key into the lock, I took the rat pieces from the pail and stuffed them into the chest pocket of my jacket. I pulled on the glove and entered Ichabod's cage.

Eyes locked on me, Ichabod shifted from one foot to the other on the platform, the log perch rolling slightly as she moved. Over the last week, Thys had got the eagle to step onto the glove from her other perch, the one by the chain-link. I faced her and pointed to the perch at the front of the cage. "Move!" The eagle rocked her weight forward and paused. "Move!" With no fanfare, Ichabod opened her wings and swooped down to the other perch. I couldn't contain myself. "All right!" I exclaimed. I smiled. I was still mystified at how I had taught Ichabod this command. She hadn't had a direct reward for following it in ages, though she always received food in the step after this one.

I walked towards the perch, watching carefully for signs of aggression. Stopping about two feet from

Ichabod, I turned my back. Keeping my eye on her over my shoulder, I slipped a piece of rat from my pocket and closed my gloved fingers around it. "Up! Up!"

The eagle stood as if carved in stone. No quiver of movement went through her body. She lowered her beak a fraction to look at the rat, then raised her eyes and gazed off into the distance. I wiggled the rat piece in my fingers. Again she dropped her eyes momentarily, then raised them to look out over the field.

"Up! Up!" Ichabod was definitely ignoring me. I backed closer to the perch, until the food was within reach of her beak. Again she lowered her head briefly, then returned to her contemplation of the world beyond the cage. I knew that repeating a word decreased the likelihood of a future response to the first command. And if I began a pattern of moving towards her, she would always wait for me to do that. Stymied and disappointed, I turned and left the cage. I had other chores to do.

The next afternoon, although it wasn't my day to work, I went to O.W.L. again. Ichabod's response was an exact replica of the day before. The story was the same the following afternoon. The third day without food, I thought as I locked the cage door behind me. That evening, worried, I phoned Terry Spring. Since the eagle was not afraid of the glove, he said, the reason she wasn't getting on it was lack of hunger. Unlike smaller birds of prey such as falcons and hawks, eagles in the wild

can easily go without food for many days at a time, and
Terry assured me that when Ichabod was hungry she'd eat
what was offered.

Not only did Ichabod seem uninterested in food on
day four, she barely acknowledged my existence. From a
foot away, I studied her feathers, her eyes, her expression.
She stood calmly, her big feet wrapped loosely over the
rough-barked perch. On a whim, I reached slowly towards her with my bare hand. The rush of blood in my
head was deafening as my heart pounded. My intention
was to feel the "meat" on either side of Ichabod's keel to
get a rough estimate of her weight. As my fingers settled
lightly on her chest feathers, Ichabod looked down and
stretched tall, leaning back slightly as if to evade my
touch. She opened her beak and gave an annoyed chitter.
Seeing no obvious aggression, however, I reached deep
within her chest feathers, my fingertips tented over her
breastbone. There was no sign of the steep drop-off that
signalled an emaciated bird. Though not fat, Ichabod
was in good weight. I removed my hand just as she made
a half-hearted feint at it with her beak. The glancing
blow knocked my hand down to my side.

I stepped back, relieved to have proof that I was
not starving the bird. I'd been told many times that falconers hunted their birds at the weight a bird in the wild
would be when deciding to look for food. Most falconers
fed their raptors completely full several times a week

and then hunted or flew their birds to the lure for food
on the other days.

On day five, I went through the familiar motions
of readying Ichabod's food, shrugging on my jacket and
walking to her cage. As I opened the door, the mood in
the cage was instantly discernible. Ichabod stood on the
perch at the chain-link, but her attention was focussed
on me. I approached her. She hunched slightly, her feathers slowly lifting over her entire body until she was twice
her normal width. I felt like laughing until I saw the look
in her eyes. It wasn't aggressive, exactly, but intent, as if
she had a job to do. I moved in a businesslike manner
to match her mood. I stopped a foot and a half from her
perch and, as I turned, shoved my hand deep into my
pocket for a piece of rat. I slid it out and into my gloved
hand in one smooth motion.

Ichabod leapt off the perch and landed with a crash
on my arm. I almost whooped aloud. She grabbed the
head of the rat, opened her wings and leapt to the air.
I gasped but hung on tight to the rat. The eagle crashed
towards the ground in a flurry, wings flailing, one foot
gripping the rat. I had the piece firmly anchored, though,
and her foot slipped free. With chilling agility, she
righted herself and flew back up, arcing around the cage
to land loudly on the perch behind me. I'd tracked her
flight and was ready with my arm outstretched. Without
hesitation, she leapt for the glove again, aiming for the

rat, this time with no intention of landing. Like fishing eagles do, she swung her legs forward neatly. Then, for a moment, all I could see was feathers. I hung on for dear life to the rat piece, and I felt a sharp wrench as Ichabod grabbed the rat and the glove, with both feet this time, and continued flying. For one crazy moment, I thought I would rise with her into the air, but instead I rocked back on my heels. Ichabod floundered, wings askew, then released the glove and rat piece and flew around my head. Panting hard, I whirled and stumbled, one foot stepping on the other. This is it, I'm done for! I thought as I righted myself, throwing my hair back from my eyes. Miraculously, there was no disturbance in the air. I looked behind me to see that the perch was vacant.

High in the corner of the platform, Ichabod stood on a stump, her beak slightly open. Keeping an eye on her, I slowly transferred the food back to my chest pocket. Ichabod looked down at the stump. Then, glancing briefly at me, she drew her beak along one wing feather. Although I was tempted to leave food for her, Terry's advice rang in my head: "Don't feed her unless you get the behaviour you want." Our encounter was over. I left the cage.

I was excited the next day as I entered Ichabod's cage and held out my glove. What kind of reception would I get? Another hit-and-run? Complete disinterest? My back to the eagle, I watched her over my shoulder as I held a large rat piece partly exposed in my gloved hand.

Ichabod remained where she was for a moment, then calmly stepped onto the glove. I stood as if an electric shock had snapped me straight. Ichabod's feet were true and square, one covering my wrist and part of my hand and the other on my forearm. I didn't attempt to grasp the jesses trailing behind her legs; I'd save that for when I planned to attach a leash. As Ichabod shifted, my breath caught in my throat. My arm stiffened as I fought to keep it still. Was she going to bate? Her wings opened slightly, and I murmured something like "Easy, easy."

Ichabod lowered her head, hunched her body and glared at me. Then she turned her eyes to the rat held in my gloved fingers. She shifted again, this time lifting the foot farthest from me and placing it fully over the food. She shuffled her other foot to follow and then lowered her head, beak reaching for the exposed flesh of the rat. Though I gripped the rat meat firmly, she pulled it clear of my glove with one sharp tug and dug the outer talons from both feet into it. My wrist wobbled, and in response to the movement, the eagle's talons pierced the rat and dug into my glove. I winced but stayed still. Ichabod's beak lowered again and, with the rat thus braced, she ripped off a long strip of meat and swallowed. Two more swallows, and the entire rat morsel was gone.

Ichabod lifted her head. Although I expected it, the punch of talons hard into my glove almost made me sway. Like an angry child out of candy, I thought. I turned towards the perch and said, "Off."

Ichabod jumped from the glove, hardly reaching
the perch before turning to face me once more. I turned
my back again and slung another piece of rat through
my gloved fingers, barely speaking the words "Up! Up!"
before she pounced. Her feet landed on the food, already
in position to brace the morsel. Three times more I asked
her onto the glove, until my pocket held no more food.

177

The third time she hesitated, and I reasoned that she was
becoming satiated. Although the last piece was smaller
than the rest, she tore it into little pieces, swallowing
each one with precision. I recognized that her daintiness
indicated a growing disinterest. As I turned to leave,
Ichabod flew up to the platform. She stood straight on
her log perch, then leaned forward and rubbed her beak
against the wood, cleaning off bits of gristle and blood.

I drove straight home from O.W.L., my excitement
barely contained. I telephoned Terry to share the details
of my day, searching for words to describe the power
and presence of Ichabod on my glove.

13

TRAINING BEGINS

I WAS STILL LOOKING for work, and
my funds were dangerously low. I had
applied for a job on a herb farm, but I was unsure how
full-time work would fit in with Ichabod's new training
regime. If I did get the job, I'd have to rise very early and
drive out to O.W.L. before my workday began. I'd taken
over some chores on the horse farm, too, and my head
spun at the idea of squeezing all of this into a day. My
horseback riding had already fallen by the wayside
despite the close proximity of the horses.

Though I had not mapped out the training regime
in detail, I planned to work towards having Ichabod fly

to my glove outside of the cage. I knew she'd have to remain tethered either to me or to a perch with climbing rope. I had found an old sawhorse near the woodpile at O.W. L., and I planned to nail a piece of thick branch to the top of it. With a heavy log set in the base, I figured the perch would be stable and secure.

The O.W. L. board of directors didn't keep track of my progress in person, though I had invited several members to watch the training. It seemed for the time being that the board was happy with my monthly written reports. Some volunteers had begun to watch from outside the cage when I called Ichabod to the glove, though, and the eagle gradually got used to this. Sometimes I even had the impression she was playing to her audience. Ichabod vocalized more when there were volunteers watching, and she spent more time with her wings fully or partly opened, as if to look more formidable. If any of the volunteers had their hands in their pockets, she'd stare fixedly at the pockets, perhaps expecting a rat to appear. Other times she had eyes only for me. Whenever she was really interested in the food I was carrying, she completely ignored the volunteers.

I learned more over the next few months about how often an eagle must eat. Unless she was hungry, Ichabod refused to jump from the perch to the glove if the distance was more than two feet. When I stood closer to her, she often stepped on and then fussed with the piece of food in my gloved fingers as if she didn't care whether she ate or not. When she was hungry, however, she'd rip off big pieces and bolt them down. With this hungry intensity came aggression. Her aggression increased gradually, sneaking up on me until I had a much different eagle on the glove.

Many falconers weighed their birds each day, and they could often tell how a day's hunting would go by the bird's weight. If the bird was too heavy, then it would perch in a tree and ignore all prey. Birds of prey that hunted on the wing, like falcons, might fly out of sight. Many falconers attached a lightweight radio transmitter to the falcon's leg to reduce the risk of losing a bird. The main method of ensuring a responsive bird, however, was to hunt only when the bird's weight was in the acceptable range. Usually, scales were rigged with perches that allowed the falconer to set the bird down for weighing in a standing position. Well-trained birds succumbed to this procedure with no more reaction than they'd have to being set on a perch in the back yard. Excitable birds would be hooded. Some smaller falcons, with their high metabolisms, could be too heavy in the morning to have an interest in hunting but be in perfect "flying weight" by that afternoon.

The only scale at O.W.L. was a large digital one located in the medical room. Since it was a human "baby scale," a bird had to be laid on its back to get a weight reading.

An O.W.L. volunteer had developed a useful cloth sleeve
with Velcro tabs to hold a bird's wings still for the brief
moment it was being weighed.

Since Ichabod was neither hood-trained nor trained
to stand quietly on a perch, for me to weigh her on a regular basis would mean subjecting her to the indignity
of being caught and laid on her back on the scale. I was
trying to secure her co-operation in the training, and
I decided that this procedure would undo any trust I'd
developed. The downside of not weighing her was that
I was unable to readily predict her behaviour. I would
find myself surprised by her hunger one day, then get no
reaction on a day when I expected a quick reaction to the
food I offered. Some foods seemed to stay in her system
longer. Rats, with their high fat content, seemed to
fill her up for days. Once she refused food for seven days
after eating a big rat, including the food I left in her
cage when I became worried. I learned as I went along.

To date, the farthest Ichabod had flown to the glove
was four feet. I realized that I needed to up the ante and
refuse her food unless she came farther. She did fly six
feet to me a few times after that, but her unpredictability
was maddening. I knew that I was too "soft," often breaking down and leaving food in the cage for her. But I was
cognizant of the information the falconers had given me
about imprinted eagles: that the aggression in a truly
hungry imprint was frightening. This fact, along with

concern for the bird's health, kept me from cutting off Ichabod's rations completely if I received no response to the glove after a few days.

I tried not to feel pressured, but I was very aware of the passage of time. The three months since the eagle had been jessed seemed to have passed in the blink of an eye, though I'd only been at it on my own for a month and a half. I was being cautious, feeling my way along. I resisted the impulse to ask Terry Spring to come out to O.W.L. weekly, knowing how busy he was. I had to do this on my own, and a part of me liked the challenge.

On good days, I was chuffed with the quick response I received from Ichabod. Because of the danger involved in the eagle flying down at me from a high perch, I showed her no food until she flew to the lower perch near the chain-link. I said "Move" whenever she sought that perch. Even if she was standing in the grass, Ichabod would turn and flap to the lower perch when I gave that command. This gave me time to ready a rat piece, turn my back and hold out my arm. Once she had landed on the perch and turned to face me, I would call her to me with "Up! Up!" Her reward for coming was the food on the glove. If the eagle attempted to come to me before heading to the lower perch, I said "No!" and showed no food. The first time I did this, I was surprised to see Ichabod fan her tail and brake in midair, turning back to the perch. The incident impressed on me how trainable Ichabod was.

Some falconers considered bald eagles stupid; some thought just the opposite. Though I knew from my work with them that the birds weren't stupid, even I was surprised at how quickly Ichabod learned. I realized she also picked up things outside the formal training. For example, I would often mutter "Wait" while I fumbled with a blood-soaked quail or struggled with my glove. One day, when Ichabod was particularly anxious for her food, I dropped it. She opened her wings to fly, and I barked out "Wait!" in frustration. She lifted her head, then settled her wings back around her body. The volunteers watching from outside the cage were stunned. I didn't let on that I was too.

Every time Ichabod pounced on the glove from her perch, landing neatly over the food, I would feel a thrill right through my bones. My arm would tingle, and I'd be unable to stop smiling. Though I always watched her leave the perch, at the last second I turned my head away to protect my face, so there was a sensation of surprise as the talons gripped my arm. Beyond these immediate sensations, there was also a deep sense of accomplishment. Sometimes I was dumbfounded by it all, not really sure what I'd done to deserve such an honour.

From a four-foot piece of climbing rope, I fashioned a leash with a carabiner on the end to slide through the slits in Ichabod's jesses. I decided to tie the leash around my waist to anchor it, and I hung the end with the carabiner alongside my thigh, handy to reach.

I knew that once Ichabod was on the glove, I would have to be careful with my bare hand. The first time I tried to pull the jesses forward into the palm of my gloved hand, I had to dodge her beak. I'd been warned by falconers that the hand reaching for the jesses could be misconstrued by the bird as an attempt to steal its food, so I was careful to wait until Ichabod was finished eating before attempting to grasp them. Even after she'd eaten, though, she struck at my bare hand with her beak, narrowly missing, and this became the routine.

One day, Ichabod grabbed the rat from my glove and then stepped up the glove towards my shoulder, gripping my elbow and bicep hard. Her head elevated by her stance, she alternated between glaring at me and lowering her head to tear at her meal. The gleaming eyes and bloody beak so close to my face strengthened my resolve. The next time Ichabod settled on the glove, before feeding her, I reached under my gloved arm and caught the trailing ends of the jesses, holding them snugly. When Ichabod tried to move up the glove, I tightened on the jesses, pulling downward, so that it was difficult for her to lift her feet. Once she was still, I released the pressure. As the eagle ate the piece of food I held for her in my gloved fingers, she lost interest in moving, and I let go of the jesses briefly, pulling the carabiner forward from the leash hanging around my waist and slipping it through the slits in the ends of the jesses. Now I had Ichabod

leashed, and the only thing remaining to do was to somehow bring the jesses and leash into the palm of my glove.

With or without a leash, jesses had to be held in the
gloved hand to allow for instant control and to keep
the bird from becoming entangled. As Ichabod finished
her food, I turned towards the lower perch. If I asked her
to get off while the leash was attached, I would be able to
adjust the jesses once she turned to face me. I could then
ask her back onto the glove with the jesses in the proper
position. It worked like a charm. Ichabod rocked my arm
as she jumped back onto the perch, and I pulled the jesses
clear of her talons. Inviting her back, I let her eat half the
food I held before furtively slipping the leather straps into
the palm of my glove and closing my hand around them.

I continued to use this new system with the eagle.
Mostly it worked well, but the jesses were artificially
shortened every time Ichabod landed on my arm with one
of the straps curled under her foot. As a result, my right
hand was crisscrossed with cuts and bruises from her
beak. I finally saw why the falconers had made her jesses
so long. As long as the jesses weren't tangled, I could slip
the carabiner through the slits just out of range of her
lunging beak.

After attaching the leash to the jesses, I would take
a few steps with the eagle on the glove. My intention was
ultimately to leave the cage in this way. I planned to set
up the sawhorse perch in the field between the care centre

and her cage. I would fasten a long length of climbing rope to the perch, so that I could transfer Ichabod to this from the leash. Then, leaving her on the perch, I would walk the distance of the rope before calling her. I envisioned Ichabod flying hundreds of feet to me, and I shivered at the imagined power of that landing. It would be a tremendous experience.

As long as Ichabod was on the glove eating, I could walk around the cage with no response from her. If she'd finished eating or had lost interest in the food, she'd bate from the glove repeatedly as I walked. I learned to stop whenever I saw signs of her being upset. Before bating, she'd drop her wings from her shoulders and lean forward; if I stopped then and spoke to her, she'd draw her wings over her back, rolling side to side as she settled. Gradually I was able to stop less often, simply slowing down when Ichabod became nervous. Some days were better than others. Some days I could only despair as the eagle crashed from the glove over and over, wings beating furiously. The bad days, I discovered, seemed related to the weather. Like horses spooking on windy days, Ichabod was super-charged in high winds. At best, she would stand lightly on the glove, wings half unfolded, paddling the air. At worst, she would dive forward repeatedly, her wings flapping furiously, bruising my face and making my eyes sting.

On one of these windy days, I learned a new lesson.

I pulled the hair from my eyes for the umpteenth time as I unsnapped the lock on Ichabod's cage. The eagle stood on the perch by the chain-link, turned away from the field to watch my entrance. The wind gusted, flattening her feathers against her body on one side. Clouds scudded across the sky behind her, giving the eagle an otherworldly appearance. With the proximity of the ocean, the weather could change quickly, and I caught a glimpse of brightness as the clouds shifted. I had tied the leash of climbing rope around my waist, and the carabiner swung against my thigh as I slipped through the door. Donning my glove and my new safety glasses, I was ready.

I walked towards Ichabod, alternating between watching the eagle and watching my footing. The grass in her cage had grown so long that it bent over. Most outdoor cages had their grass cut regularly, the occupants temporarily removed or shooed into another cage. But because Ichabod ate all of her food immediately, I didn't have to look for scraps in the tall grass, and I liked how it made ground logs and branches into smooth hummocks of green.

The bit of flattened grass where I always stood accepted my feet perfectly as I swivelled into place, my back to the eagle. My right hand groped for a rat piece, fingers slipping over the blood-slick meat. Unexpectedly, I heard a whoosh. I was slow to compute that the eagle was in the air. My mouth didn't form the word "Wait."

Instead, I straightened my gloved arm hurriedly and slapped the meat into my palm. As the bird's wings swept closer, I turned my face away for the landing. Suddenly the hair rose on the back of my neck. Something wasn't right. As the wind buffetted both sides of my head, I realized too late what it was. Ichabod wasn't making for the glove.

I felt the white-hot puncture in my scalp as a big foot wrapped around the back of my head. I sensed the other foot swinging near the side of my neck. Ichabod's wings crashed around my head and shoulders, and my safety glasses were flicked away. Instinctively, I bent my gloved elbow and chucked the meat. Ichabod pushed off my head as if it were a perch and followed the food. The wings flapping around my head were gone. I heard the grass rustle as she landed on the food, then all was quiet. My head was throbbing, and I became aware of a great roaring: blood pounding under the bones of my skull. I suddenly realized with absolute certainty that the eagle must not eat the meat. If she did, she'd have received a reward for attacking me. Half blind from the blood running down my scalp, I advanced on her fast. She looked up in surprise, then fiercely mantled the rat piece, shielding her feet from my eyes with her wings. I felt scared, reckless and angry all at once.

"MOVE!" I shouted. My sneakers were two feet from the bird. Thrown off by the speed of my approach and probably my furious body language, she let loose an anguished caw and flew to her platform, sans meat. I picked it up quickly and left the cage.

Once outside, I leaned on her door. Blood pounded in my ears. I touched my scalp gingerly and felt the already congealing lumps of blood and twisted hair. Probing further, I found that one spot near the top of my head was still seeping. A spider web of sticky blood crisscrossed my cheek.

I stood still until the throbbing in my skull subsided. I wanted to hide the injury from people in the care centre, but when I looked at my watch, I thought it likely that everyone else had already left. The volunteers wouldn't understand that the human-imprinted eagle— unlike Lucy, imprinted to her own kind—was not afraid of arguing with people to get her way. I'd sensed that many people doubted I could train Ichabod, and though I knew it was not uncommon for eagle falconers to get hurt, it would go against me if others at the centre knew that.

Out back of the care centre, I ran a hose over a towel I'd found and wiped the blood from my face and forehead. Entering O.W.L., I was relieved to see only the supervisor of the day, who was a friend. She matter-of-factly indicated the medical room as a destination, and I sat on a stool while she pulled the hair from my scalp wounds and cleaned the punctures with peroxide.

My hands shook slightly as I drove home. How could I fly Ichabod to the glove if at any time she might decide to grab my head or face? I shuddered at what could have happened. My confidence in my work had suffered a blow, and I felt the slow crawl of fear along my spine as I remembered what the falconers had said about imprinted eagles. I felt strangely betrayed. In getting Ichabod to trust me, I had begun to trust her. I chided myself. From my work with horses, I should know better than to take this personally. The prey drive of an eagle, like the flight response in a horse, is deeply ingrained. I remembered the satisfaction of Ichabod's neat landings, the pleasurable sensation of those big feet wrapped around my forearm.

I called Terry when I got home. He wasn't surprised by the incident, and he suggested that I stand with my back against something whenever I flew Ichabod loose in the cage. His advice calmed me. I went to bed thinking that the large square roof-support post in Ichabod's cage might do the trick.

_14_

FIELDWORK

L IKE A HERD of science-fiction monsters, giant red engines idled near the parking lot of the rail yard. Their rumbling voices were punctuated by unnerving spits of air.

My falconer friend Terry Spring worked as a locomotive engineer for Canadian Pacific Railway. During our phone call, he had told me that the CPR was hiring brakemen and encouraged me to hand in a résumé. I reviewed the little I knew about trains as I walked down the long line of vehicles in the employee parking lot: they were huge, and they blocked crossings when you least expected them to. I remembered, as a teenager, keeping a sharp eye out for trains while riding horses in Winnipeg. I had to cross a set of tracks to reach the Assiniboine forest, and a far-off whistle was guaranteed to make my heart pound as I tried to manoeuvre my skittish horse over the tracks and as far from the impending train as possible.

By thinking of Terry, red-eyed but cheerful as he stood with his falcon after piloting a late-night train through the Fraser Canyon, I reasoned away my misgivings. Terry was able to keep his rail job and still have time to fly and care for a large number of falcons, not to mention performing for the public at outdoor demonstrations with his birds. The need for a steady income moved my reluctant feet towards the doorway of the yard office.

One of the engines in the group to my left revved suddenly, the spits of air coming faster. I strained to see a human head up in the cab, but the red monster's small windows were empty. Despite the absence of an engineer, I feared that any minute the locomotive would jolt into motion. Then, just as suddenly, the engine changed timbre and returned to a deep, slow idle that vibrated in my chest. I gave the locomotive one more suspicious glance before turning towards the office steps. Inside, I was directed to a manager's office, where I had a brief conversation with someone before pulling my résumé out of my small leather binder.

A few days later I received a call from Canadian Pacific, asking me to appear at 3:00 A.M. at a hotel near the yard office. Three A.M.! Terry said it was a test to see if the fifty people selected in the first round would show up on time. This group of hopefuls would eventually be reduced through interviews to between ten and twelve.

In the wee hours of the morning, with the rest of the weary group of fifty, I listened to all the reasons why I wouldn't want a railway career: on-call status twenty-four hours a day, seven days a week; frequent layoffs; outside work in bad weather. After that, we were asked to fill out an application that included a paragraph stating why we were interested in working for the railway. From these applications, twenty-five candidates would be chosen for interviews. Someone called me a few days later. I'd made it to the second round.

In the weeks following my scalp injury, I settled into a new routine with Ichabod. I began to stand with my back to the roof-support post, using the "Wait" command to allow myself enough time to get there. Typically, I'd open the cage door and Ichabod would fly to the perch by the chain-link, sitting there expectantly. I'd tell her to wait as I walked towards the post, which was fifteen feet from the door in her direction. I glanced at her occasionally, but I kept my eyes mostly on the ground. If I tripped, I knew Ichabod would attack me. I could see the urge to fly at me quiver through her as I took the last few steps. I'd keep my strides even and casual, though my pulse raced. Reaching the post, I'd

pivot and then ask her to the glove with the "Up! Up!"
command.

Once the eagle had landed, was leashed and had
begun to eat, I would walk towards the cage door, piec-
ing together the journey that would soon take us from
the cage to the field. As the time I spent carrying the
eagle increased, my left arm would grow very tired. After
fifteen minutes, it would begin to sag. I started lifting
weights at home to strengthen it.

I'd slowly been learning that the amount of food I fed
Ichabod affected both her behaviour and her willingness
to accept new things. If I fed her too small a piece of food,
she'd bate from the glove once she lifted her head from
eating and realized we were nearing the cage door. As the
training progressed, I began to feed her large pieces so that
we could reach the door and even open it without incident.

Walking through the door turned out to be a whole
new ballgame. The small opening worried the eagle.
If she was really hungry, I could give her another piece
of meat to occupy her while we were stepping through.
If she wasn't hungry, however, she'd look up from the
food, realize our location, twist around and dive from the
glove in a great crash of wings towards the interior of
the cage. Using the jesses, I'd swing her away from the
door frame to keep her wings from injury.

Ichabod's fear of the doorway was greater than all but
the strongest hunger, but it was a delicate balance to get

her hungry enough for success with the door but not so hungry that she became hyper-aggressive. For health reasons, I couldn't keep her at flying weight for days on end, so I fed her every time we came near the doorway and then, if I judged her receptive, walked her right through. Our progress was steady but slow. The six-month time frame specified by O.W.L.'s board of directors for Ichabod's training had long since passed, though I'd heard nothing from them other than confirmation of receiving my monthly reports. I kept my head down and tried to make up for lost time by coming to O.W.L. daily, despite the strain on my pocketbook.

Finally one day when I walked through the cage door, Ichabod stayed on the glove with only a trace of her previous tension. I was thrilled. As she continued to remain calm on the glove going through the doorway, I reduced the amount of food I gave her to keep her there. It was important to move smoothly at all times, though, since any abrupt movement resulted in a leap from my arm.

Despite the increased strength in my left arm, I still found anything more than twenty minutes of holding my arm out for the eleven-pound eagle to be a challenge, especially if she was bating. I always found the strength to continue, but my arm ached from the weight combined with the gripping talons. I was heartened when Terry reassured me that falconers tire from carrying a four-pound bird close to their bodies.

One morning Ichabod and I walked through the open door, rounded the side of the bank of cages and moved to the field behind the care centre. Ichabod lifted her head high, peering with interest at her new view. With excitement coursing through me, I eyed the sawhorse perch standing ready for the next phase of our training.

During the next few sessions, I reduced further the amount of food I fed the eagle in the cage and increased what I fed her once we reached the field. I wanted to get to a point where I'd feed her only in the field. I reasoned that I was in most danger of an attack while she was loose in the cage. I hoped eliminating the feeding there would reduce that risk. Once Ichabod was on a leash or tethered in some way, I was safer. Over the course of a week, I manipulated her food supply to sharpen her interest for our first session of coming to the glove from the sawhorse perch.

At last the day came. After walking with Ichabod from the cage into the field, I asked her to step off the glove onto the sawhorse perch. I held my breath as she hesitated. An unseen bird in a nearby cage flapped its wings, and I felt tension coil through the eagle. After a minute, Ichabod hopped down from my glove to the sawhorse perch. Just as I turned away to reach for food, she leapt back onto the glove.

Ichabod inclined her head and peered at me with what seemed like a playful expression. I felt my chest swell with emotion at the sight. Is this right? she seemed to be asking. I turned back to the perch and said, "Off!" The eagle jumped to the sawhorse perch, then twisted back to face me. This time, I was ready with her food. At my "Up! Up!" she landed back on the glove and gripped the rat piece with one foot, barely settling before gulping down the food in one swallow. Her talons bit into the leather, and suddenly she was all business. Three more times I called her to the glove from the extent of the leash, and she responded instantly.

As we walked back to her cage, Ichabod stood lightly on the glove, wings half opened. Because she wasn't distracted by food, her nervousness was apparent as we rounded the end of the cage heading for the doorway. I kept my breathing steady with effort. When we slipped through the door without incident, I heaved a sigh of relief.

Soon afterwards, I invited Terry to O.W.L. to observe the training. I had decided I would transfer Ichabod to the long line attached to the sawhorse for this session, flying her to me over a greater distance than she'd ever covered before.

Ichabod stood ready on her perch as I entered the cage that afternoon. A crescent of space curved between her body and her wings. She lifted her wings further from her body, displacing air in shallow scooping motions. I hurried to the support post and put my back to it. I lifted my elbow clear of my body, and as I dropped my gloved forearm level, a taloned foot grabbed it where it narrowed. Ichabod's free foot swung around to drop beside the other, enclosing my wrist and the back of my hand with a crunch. My arm ached from hand to mid-forearm. No rat piece poked from my hand, and Ichabod didn't bother to look for one. She'd gotten used to the idea that the food rewards began once we were out in the field. In just a few short sessions, she'd mastered this system, and her swiftness to my glove in the cage was amazing.

After pulling the jesses through my glove and holding them firmly, I attached the leash. I pulled the carabiner through the slits quickly, ever mindful of the eagle's talons close to my bare fingers. I tugged on the leash to double-check that I'd tied it firmly around my waist. Ichabod's wings hung open, cloaking my arm. She refused to close them when we reached the cage door, so I had to seesaw through the doorway, slipping first one wing through and then the other in a sideways motion.

Terry stood near the sawhorse perch, and Ichabod's head snapped erect when she saw him. He held the purple climbing rope in his hand. It was already fastened to the sawhorse, and he double-checked the climbing knot before threading the rope through his hand. When he came to the carabiner, his fingers checked that knot as well. All seemed to be in order. As we drew closer, Terry said, "She's in yarak."

Ichabod in yarak was impressive, and I could see
Terry admiring her. She always seemed larger at those
times, her feathers puffed out from her body. The feathers
at the back of her head lifted so that they mimicked the
streamlined lift on the racing helmets bicyclists wear.
Her eyes glittered as if she was plugged into a socket.

I was surprised by the yarak, because I had fed Ichabod a medium-sized portion of food just the day before.
Today was cold and windy, though, and I surmised that
the change in the weather from yesterday's heat had
brought on her single-minded interest in killing. I'd
noticed that the resident raptors at o.w.l. often ate
more during a cold snap.

I'd been reasonably sure that Ichabod would fly to
my glove today, but now that she was in yarak, there was
no question about it. The unknown factor was what she
would do to me when she landed. I'd never had such an
intense eagle on the glove before. Usually she loosened
her grip after we'd walked a few steps, but today her feet
continued to grasp my arm as if it was a hard-won prize.

I stood close to the sawhorse. Terry handed me the
carabiner he was holding, with the purple climbing rope
trailing behind. I pulled the small carabiner at the end of
Ichabod's leash forward. I slipped the larger carabiner
through the slits in her jesses, so that for a moment she
was attached to both my waist leash and the perch line.
Then I disconnected the leash and let it hang against
my thigh.

Holding the jesses and the rope, I faced the sawhorse perch and gave the usual command: "Off." Ichabod croaked, then reared her head back over her shoulders and hissed, her eyes meeting mine. I felt her gaze hot on my skin. I stood still for a minute, then lowered my arm slightly, as if to motivate her to the perch. She gave another guttural croak, then leapt to the sawhorse.

I dropped the rope and backed away quickly as she settled. Turning my back to her at the rope's length of twelve feet, I reached for a piece of quail from my pocket.

My left arm straightened from my body, the quail in my hand. I felt the eagle leave the perch before I heard or saw anything. I forgot about Terry watching as I waited for the wide wings to enclose me, the taloned feet to slam into the glove. Time seemed to slow. I turned my head for a glimpse. Ichabod's tail was fanned, her wings half folded, her feet swinging forward. She hunched in the air just before she landed, head and feet close together. With the extra distance, I had extra time to appreciate the spectacle of the eagle coming in for a landing. I saw her feet as I didn't normally see them, from the underside: three top toes fully extended, the thick bottom one already curling forward in a gripping action. I turned my head away.

My breath released in a whoosh as the full impact of the eagle's feet and body hit me. I stumbled forward, shocked by the force of her landing. My eyes watered as she clamped onto my arm. The eagle snaked her head towards the piece of quail held tightly in my gloved fingers. Stunned that her landing hadn't shaken the food loose, I stood quiet, overwhelmed by her power. I didn't know whether to laugh or cry.

I turned towards Terry, managing to speak in a normal tone. He responded positively, and I replied with words that revealed nothing of how I felt. I didn't know how to express this experience, and I had a sudden intense need for privacy.

The closest I'd come to this feeling was watching horses running to the first turn at the racetrack. My throat would tighten and my eyes tear as the creatures stretched their bodies low, propelling themselves forward. The fierce rhythm of hooves biting the ground and the open red-rimmed nostrils sucking up great draughts of air captivated me.

Ichabod held me pinned to the earth, her big wings lowered but half open, ready to launch her to the sky. I felt a humming over my skin. The last of the tingling backwash of power spiralled away as the eagle loosened her grip slightly. It was time to return her to the perch for another flight to the glove. My legs shook as I walked to the sawhorse, eagle towering beside me.

15

ICHABOD IN FLIGHT

T HROUGH SOME FRIENDS, I met
a woman who was looking for someone
to live in the ground-level suite of her farmhouse. If the
tenant was also willing to take care of the woman's children a few times a week, the rent on the suite would be
reduced. Though I was happy where I currently lived, the
reduced-rent idea was attractive. I went to see the apartment. The farm was near the border on a high and dry five
acres, a large portion of it forest. An old barn housed the
woman's two horses. From the apartment porch I'd have a
view of the rolling Hazelmere valley. The only drawback
was that the married couple who owned the farm

intended to demolish the house sometime over the next year to build their dream home on the site. Nonetheless, the opportunity to live alone in an affordable manner was too great to pass up. I decided to move.

Through a chance encounter shortly afterwards, I found myself the owner of a large dog. My new landlady agreed to my request to have the dog live with me, and so Moon Dog, a Rottweiler/Lab/shepherd cross, came to stay. She established herself in my life as friend and protector. She was wonderful with children, too, which pleased my new neighbours. I cleaned stalls for the land-lady for a little extra money, and Moon Dog began to accompany me, discovering a passion for hunting mice.

I continued my work with Ichabod outside of the cage. I'd become proficient at negotiating the doorway smoothly, and our walk to the field was routine. Ichabod seemed to like the field sessions. She'd lean forward as we approached the corner of the cages, craning to see around the building and gripping the glove hard.

One day I stood in the field at O.W.L. watching a plane come in for a landing at Boundary Bay. The pilot was flying at a slight angle, with the plane's flaps de-ployed. As he disappeared from sight behind the shrubs and brambles, I thought about Ichabod's "flaps," the spread feathers of her tail and wings. Flight had begun to interest me more and more as the eagle flew greater distances to me across the field behind the centre.

I noticed how different kinds of wind affected her progress. A strong tailwind skated her sideways, making her landings precarious. For this reason, unless she was really hungry, she was reluctant to fly in a straight line to my glove when the wind was blowing from behind. She would fuss on the sawhorse perch, wanting to face me but uncomfortable with the wind lifting her tail. When the wind was blowing towards her, Ichabod flapped harder as she flew but seemed otherwise unaffected. When the wind hit her from the side, she flew awkwardly, wings flapping unevenly as she was blown off her flight path. I'd read that the downward thrust was the main power source for a bird's flight, with the pectoral muscles much better developed than the tendons and muscles that raised the wing. I sought out books on the mechanics of bird flight, and I marvelled at the variety of flight styles, each tailor-made for a particular escape or hunting strategy.

By now, I'd increased the distance Ichabod flew to me to twenty feet, and I had even more time to observe her as she came towards me: three wing-flaps' worth. It took her four seconds to reach me on average, depending on the wind and her attitude. At the last possible split-second before she landed, I'd turn my face away to feel the rush of air against my cheek and ear. Each time I caught a glimpse of her feet reaching for my glove, a shot of fear would go through me.

After Ichabod had landed, I captured the climbing rope and carabiner with my right hand while she tore at the food I held in my gloved hand. As she ate, I'd walk back towards the perch. Usually, at the command "Off," she'd leap back to the perch and then spin around to face me. Turning my back on her didn't seem smart, so I'd walk quickly to the edge of her range, looking constantly over my shoulder.

Some days, no matter what I did, the eagle was determined to follow me off the perch. One late-summer afternoon she overflew me. As the rope pulled tight, she ricocheted around my opposite side, wrapping me in the rope. I tried to duck out from under it, but I was truly tangled. I twisted to locate Ichabod, feeling something brushing my hips. Ichabod was hanging upside down from the rope, her talons at my waist level. She opened her wings and spun herself around, trying to fly up to the highest point, my head. Luckily, she only made it as far as my chest. I had a sudden vision of an eagle gripping my lapel with one foot and bunching up my jacket with the other, shaking me down like a gangster for money owed. Ichabod's head reared far above mine, and the musty smell of old blood and carrion filled my nose. I stood frozen for a moment, my face all but buried in the small brown feathers of her stomach.

I managed to extricate myself by ducking under the rope and spinning in a half circle. I grasped the eagle's legs, one in each hand, and made my way to the sawhorse, heart thumping. But there I dithered. Ichabod's feet were still clutching my jacket. I didn't want to let go of either leg and have her try to climb up my face. Finally, I screwed up enough courage to release one ankle, reach rapidly into my pocket and place a piece of rat on the sawhorse. Ichabod let go at once to pounce on the food.

As she ate, I surveyed my torn lapel and the more sinister holes in my jacket and T-shirt. I was lucky Ichabod had come out of yarak, or I'd be missing half my face. Yarak was a state in which the eagle became "other," something so wild and foreign it was hard not to quake with fear and throw as much food at her as she could gobble down. Occasionally I was able to balance her food intake so that the eagle on my glove was keen but not in full yarak, but this was not often. Several times a week I flew her in yarak, with her attitude lessening as she ate. Those times I returned her to her cage with "one more flight left in her," so as to have a successful session the next day. On the other days of the week, I fed her as much as she would come to me for. If I got no response, I would gather her up and return her to her cage, then skip feeding her the next day. Some days I didn't feel I had enough concentration to deal with Ichabod in full yarak. If I wasn't mentally or physically prepared, I could make a mistake that would get me badly injured. During those sessions, I would give the eagle a large piece of food on her first short flight to take the edge off, then ask her onto the glove for short hops, feeding her full quickly.

No two flights were exactly alike. Once a gust lifted

her straight up and she flew down at the glove, the wind whistling through her primary feathers. Sometimes the sun appeared to swallow her, and I'd look back over my shoulder to see orange lozenges of brightness hiding her head momentarily or blotting out her legs so that she seemed to hover above the perch. I'd call her to the glove and she'd once again take solid form.

One afternoon, I called her to the glove and turned away as usual at the last minute, bracing myself for her landing. But after a few seconds there was only silence. I'd seen her aloft, but no yellow feet reached for my leather-clad arm. For a moment, I wondered if the rope had snapped and I had lost her. I turned to look, my eyes flicking to the sky, then back down again.

Ichabod stood on the ground about ten feet away. Had I dropped food there earlier? But she wasn't eating. I could see her talons, sharply etched against the newly mown grass.

"What are you up to?" I muttered aloud.

The eagle turned her head sideways and gave me her "cute" look.

"I guess these last few feet were too much effort?"

Ichabod jerked her head to the left, twisting it sideways. There was nothing cute about her look now. Her eyes were locked on the grass. Her head bobbed as she tracked some movement in a patch of grass the mower had missed.

In a flash of feathers, the eagle opened her wings. I stood ready to throw out my arm if she came my way. But she remained on the ground, wings outspread like a cape. She stretched to her full height and stood poised, reminding me of a Spanish dancer preparing for a furious flamenco. After a moment, Ichabod pounced on the rough grass. I couldn't see what had inspired the attack. She stood frozen in her new position, this time with her head arched back and her wings dropped. Her long brown primary feathers were drawn forward to cover her feet, and her eyes met mine.

"What have you got?" I said. I started to walk towards her.

Crak, crak, crak, she cried. She dropped her gaze. I stepped closer. She whipped her head up, looked straight at me and rapped out again, *Crak, crak, crak.* As I leaned closer, a snake whipped its body around her ankle. Ichabod had covered its head with her foot.

Backing away, I watched her strip long ribbons of meat from the snake. I moved towards her as she finished, and just as I bent carefully to offer the glove, she leaned forward and swiped her beak back and forth across my running shoe, wiping the excess blood and gore onto the cracked leather. She stepped on the glove very sedately after that. Since she showed no interest in my offerings of food, I returned her to her cage.

During one of our training sessions, as I tried yet again to evade Ichabod's beak while attaching the leash,

I thought how easily Terry Spring handled the jesses of his falcons. I'd even seen him attach a radio transmitter to Quest's leg. Terry's hands were large and strong from outdoor work, but they carried few scars. I looked ruefully at my own right hand as I tried for the third time to slip the leash carabiner through the slits in the end of Ichabod's jesses. My hand was covered with little inden-tations and white scars from the eagle's bites. Usually when her beak came forward in a lunge, my hand was almost beyond reach, and she only scraped it shallowly. As long as the jesses were straight, I could keep my hand out of range. But often at least one of them was twisted a little or partially bound up under Ichabod's feet. When Ichabod was fully in yarak, I was very aware of the possibility of her "footing" me. Though she hadn't yet tried to grab my bare hand with her talons, I watched carefully for signs she was about to. I'd take the bites over being footed any day. After she'd eaten, though, I could swivel the soft leather anklets around her legs, test-ing their fit. Her scaly yellow feet felt smoother than I expected.

On hot days, I'd taken to hanging a spray bottle from the climbing-rope leash around my waist. I'd spray Ichabod's feet with it, cooling her down as we worked. I'd mist her body, too, and she often made drinking motions with her beak if water was sprayed near her head. Sometimes she lunged at the spray bottle, sending it fly-ing. She'd look at me with a self-satisfied air afterwards.

I invited O.W.L. volunteers to watch Ichabod fly in the back field as long as they stayed out of range. I had still heard nothing from the board of directors. Perhaps by now I had proven the eagle was trainable? The situation made me nervous, but most of the time I was too caught up in my experiences with the bird to pay attention to my worries. Once Ichabod was done flying and I'd transferred her from the creance to my waist leash, I allowed the volunteers to come closer. I'd weave the eagle's jesses through my fingers, so that if she bated she couldn't travel far. For the most part she was mannerly, assuming the attitude of a queen being admired by her subjects. If someone became a little too comfortable when leaning forward to look at Ichabod's equipment, however, the crest on the back of her head would rise. Once a volunteer holding the spray bottle inadvertently drilled Ichabod in the face with a jet of water. The bird lunged, knocking the bottle to the ground and just missing the volunteer's hand.

Though I continued to lift weights to increase the strength and steadiness of my left arm, my arm still got very tired. If I had Ichabod out for a while, I would need to rest my arm against something periodically or sit down with it supported. At first Ichbabod disliked being down low, and she would bate. I compromised by holding her with my arm resting on a raised knee as I sat in the grass, her jesses pulled tight, and after a while she adapted. Sometimes a group of volunteers would sit with

210

CONVERSATIONS WITH AN EAGLE

me. Ichabod's behaviour was exemplary. She would gravely contemplate her "followers" from her slightly raised vantage point.

One day, Terry Spring stood in my place in the field and called Ichabod to the glove. I stood out of the creance's range and watched them work. It was wonderful to observe her flying to the glove the whole way, not having to turn away as she landed. Her wings darkened the sky as she braked. Her tail fanned and her legs dangled for a moment before she swung decisively forward to grab the glove. She was not merely alighting on it but actively and aggressively grabbing the leather.

Seconds after she landed, Terry had her jesses and the attached rope in his grasp. Ichabod leapt for his face. She was brought up short by his expert hold, however, and the attack was foiled. I stood dumbfounded. She had never tried that on me. Terry explained later that Ichabod was probably a one-person bird. Apparently it was not unusual for eagles to form an attachment to the person they dealt with most often. Falcons did this too, I knew. But they were nowhere near as dangerous or unpredictable as an imprinted bald eagle.

16

SETBACK

I WAITED BY the switch along a stretch
of rail near the highway. A dried-up
starfish lay near the tip of my steel-toed boot, reminding
me of how close to the ocean I was. The Barnet Inlet was
only a hundred feet away, but the lapping of water
against rock was drowned out by the sounds of metal on
metal. The radio microphone clipped to the bib of my
striped coveralls crackled, and then I heard my conductor
give his instructions. The giant tank cars beside me
creaked. Air hissed through the hoses between them as
the engineer, ten cars away, charged the brake pipe with
air. The railcars jerked forward, engines chugging as the
cars were pulled clear of the switch.

I depressed the button on my mike and spoke to the engineer. For a few seconds the black cars continued moving, then they slowed and came to a gentle stop, the engineer drawing air from the brake pipe to set the brake shoes against the wheels. I cranked the handle on the switch and watched the switch points slip smoothly over, creating a new course for the wheels to follow. The cars jostled and clanked, the draw bars connecting them extending until the slack had run out. Everything had settled to stillness just as I gave the command to back up. I used my mike again, telling the conductor, out of sight back in the "tank farm," that the railcars were coming his way. Then I settled in to wait again, the ocean scent thick in my nostrils. I tucked the tiny twisted starfish into my pocket.

It was late winter, and I was close to the end of my brakeman training with CPR. I'd put in four months of practical and classroom time, and there were only a few more tests before graduation. I enjoyed the work, I'd discovered. Being in the outdoors was a large part of it, but there was also something compelling about the powerful engines and something satisfying in figuring out the most efficient way to switch the railcars into order. Since the work was so foreign to my experience, it was never boring. I saw employees with twenty years under their belts who were still learning.

There was danger at the railway also, and I found I liked the risk and drama of mountains of metal slipping along thin steel rails. I liked working outside at night, watching owls hunt mice around the grain cars. Railway workers had their own community, and sometimes it felt a little like family. Driving to O.W.L., I no longer dreaded the whistle of an oncoming coal train likely to block my path. Instead, I watched the cab for people I knew and sat relaxed in my car, listening to the hum of wheels on rail. It was the sound that had come to mean my livelihood.

That spring I began work as a CPR brakeman. I worked on call, usually in a subordinate position to the foreman. I was paid a set rate every week, with the option to work more hours for extra money. Because night and late-afternoon shifts were common, there was lots of time to work with Ichabod. One day as I walked to her cage, I noticed some piles of lumber near her field perch. I'd heard from other volunteers that a new cage was being built between Ichabod's section and the older flight cages across the field. I moved the sawhorse perch clear of the lumber and thought no more of it.

The farmhouse where I lived was due to be torn down soon. Yet again, I would have to move. While driving through nearby Cloverdale, I stopped to check the notice board at a shop that sold saddles and other horseback-riding equipment. There was one ad for shared accommodation on a horse farm in south Surrey. I phoned from the nearest pay phone and set up an appointment for later that day.

The south Surrey house had four bedrooms and lots of living space. The lot was six acres, with a barn and horse fields out the back. The tenants seemed friendly and easygoing. I had brought Moon Dog along to meet them, and they liked her immediately. I made arrangements to move in.

I saw Ichabod as often as I could, at least every second day. She flew to me consistently now. On one occasion, I stood enthralled in the middle of the field, seeing the elongated shadow of my body against the grass with wings sprouting from my shoulders as if I were a mythical being. Ichabod would crow with triumph as she grasped the glove upon landing. She was usually fierce but businesslike in the cage while I fastened her jesses to the leash. Outside the cage, she would lean forward eagerly whenever her sawhorse perch came into view.

Several volunteers regularly attended Ichabod's flying sessions. I'd sit on the grass with them afterwards, eagle on my arm, and we'd talk about raptors. I felt a kinship with these young men and women who were as content to bask in Ichabod's presence as I was. The director at O.W. L. had asked me to train someone to help me with the eagle, but given Terry's observation that Ichabod was a one-person bird, I didn't think it would be possible. Occasionally, one of the supervisors would make a negative comment about the fact that only I could deal with Ichabod. I was troubled by the emphasis on this, when the eagle's training was going so well. I invariably answered by saying that I was committed to Ichabod and would make myself available for any eventual educational work that involved her.

One day, the CP Rail crew office contacted me to say they'd like me to take conductor training. This would allow me to be both a foreman in the yard and a conductor in charge of freight trains. Laden with rule books, I made my way to my first class in late spring. Like brakeman training, it would be a combination of classroom and practical time, four months in total. With the days becoming longer at this time of year, I'd be able to continue my work with Ichabod without much change.

On an afternoon in early summer, before I could make my way to Ichabod's cage, O.W.L.'s director told me that work on the new cage was about to begin. I couldn't fly Ichabod in the field until the work was completed, she said, citing safety concerns for both the workers and the bird. I suggested that I find a new flight corridor on the O.W.L. grounds, but she asked me to keep the eagle in her cage for the time being.

I was worried at the thought of "grounding" the eagle. I would miss the excitement and the interaction. And what about Ichabod? How would she feel about being confined to a cage again for twenty-four hours a day? I hoped I was overreacting, though. After all, how long could it take to build a cage?

I didn't notice any difference in the eagle at first. I'd
usually feed her a small piece of rat through the chain-link
before I walked around behind her cage to the door. While
she finished the food, I'd enter and position myself at the
support post. When she lifted her head, I'd purse my lips
and whistle for her, five short bursts, with the fifth dropping in pitch. This was something new I was trying, and
it seemed to work well. After a few sessions, I switched
to a plastic whistle in order to get a louder sound. Ichabod
would fly towards me and bind to the glove. I'd walk her
back to her perch while she ate another piece of rat, ask
her to jump to the branch, then make my way quickly
back to the post for another go. Sometimes I attached the
leash, then hopped her to the glove for a few short flights
the length of it. Often, at the end of our session, I sat
on a low stump with Ichabod on my glove and spoke to
her about anything that came to mind.

Other times Ichabod and I would "play catch." I'd
feed her a small morsel before I entered the cage. Then,
while she was occupied, I'd throw a piece of food in the air
and blow on a plastic whistle. The eagle would fly straight
up and snatch the food in the air, crowing triumphantly.
Sometimes she'd swoop down on it instead, snatching
it with a sideways swing of her legs or a one-footed grab.

Construction on the new cage proceeded in fits
and starts. Before I knew it, three months had slipped by.
One late afternoon, I decided to approach Ichabod's cage

from behind the scraggly fir trees planted along the chain-link, so that I could watch her without being seen. She moved restlessly on her perch. I noticed with a start that her head was now almost completely white. Like a mother not noticing her kid growing because she's right in front of her, I thought. And when had her eyes changed completely to cool lemon? No, not lemon, something harder, maybe topaz. As she inclined her head, tiny white cowl feathers made a scalloped edge along her brown shoulders.

Something was crawling along the bark at her feet. The eagle watched it intently, then grabbed with her foot, ripping up a large chunk of bark and, undoubtedly, a hapless insect. I inched closer, surprised that Ichabod hadn't noticed me yet. She stood frozen now on the perch, looking out across the field, and I turned to see what had riveted her. A volunteer swung a dead rat back and forth as he spoke to a man with a wheelbarrow. Ichabod's head was lowered, and her eyes were locked on the volunteer. They looked feral, blazing with energy. As I wondered if the volunteer could feel her gaze, I felt a funny quiver in my stomach. I knew this creature as well as a human can know any wild animal or bird, yet her cold concentration gave me a frisson of fear. Her predatory nature was evident in her every action and look. Yet she exhibited a kind of trust and comfort around me that could be taken for affection. I always felt honoured by this trust, just as I did when a horse I was leading chose to follow me past a "scary monster" that was usually a rock hidden in the grass.

I moved sideways into plain sight. Ichabod's head snapped towards me, the crest rising on the back of her head. As I reached into my pocket and pulled out a small rat, her eyes widened. I slipped the rat through the chain-link, and it hit the ground the same time she did. She took the food up to the platform, but instead of swallowing it whole, as I expected, she held it between her feet, worrying it with her beak. Catching me looking, she let loose a high-pitched cry, then a guttural croaking. Her head was low, eyes locked on mine.

It was unusual behaviour. The fierceness I'd observed in her as she watched the volunteer was usually diminished once I gave her some food. But this time she was playing with it. My stomach tingled again, and I unlocked the door to the cage quietly, feeling an absurd need for stealth. As I stepped inside, I heard the loud thump of the log rocking as Ichabod took to the air.

I flung my arm out at the same time a big foot grabbed my left shoulder. The eagle's other foot closed tightly around my left elbow. Her wings lashed the air above me. I could see the thick brown length of her thigh as I reared my head back and away. My ungloved right hand swung up, palm leading, and I pushed the heel of it hard into her thigh, rocking the shoulder she gripped at the same time. I could feel her surprise. Her wings buffeted my head, their rhythm haphazard, then she released her grip and flew away.

Breathing hard, I took stock. Bare hand not maimed, no blood; jacket and sweatshirt ripped at the shoulder, but no white-hot pain. I stepped briskly towards the square post, listening for Ichabod. To catch my breath, I leaned my head against the post momentarily and looked back towards the platform. There she was, poised on the log and swaying forward slightly.

I slipped my right hand into my pocket and felt the yielding flesh of a rat. With a shaking hand, I slung the rat through my gloved fingers and called, "Up! Up!"

Ichabod dropped from the platform. One flap of wings, and then her landing gear swung forward, giant feet opening like terrible yellow flowers. She's too high, part of my brain screamed. As she dipped down through the air, I locked my eyes on those swinging legs and thrust my gloved arm up to meet them. At the last minute, she flew past me. I readied myself for a frontal assault, raising my arm to block as she spun agilely in the air. Instead, she powered past again. I heard her land hard behind me, rocking the stump on the platform. I backed hastily from the cage. My last glimpse of Ichabod revealed her reaching down to the rat still draped on the edge of the platform.

Over the next few weeks, the eagle's intensity forced me to approach her with much more caution than usual.

As I walked to her cage, I would look over at the half-completed cage with annoyance. The sawhorse perch looked abandoned, and one day I noticed that the creance line was missing from it. How long had it been gone? With a start, I realized that it was almost four months since Ichabod had left the cage; I'd be graduating from conductor training in a couple of days.

I searched the grass nearby for the bright purple rope, to no avail. Then, glancing up at the roof of the new cage, I saw my flying line attached to a bundle of construction material. The workers were using it to haul heavy materials to the roof. In an instant, my frustration at being thwarted in the training with Ichabod caught up to me. I stood furiously clenching and unclenching my fists. I consciously slowed my breathing after a minute, recognizing that the workers could have no idea of what the rope was really for, what it meant to me.

I found a ladder and climbed onto the roof of the cage, my progress made precarious by the trembling in my legs. The load of roof materials seemed stable on its own, so I inched farther up the ladder and reached for the knots in the climbing rope. My fingers shook as I untied them. By the time I had reached the ground with the coil of line in my hand, I felt drained. Instead of reattaching it to the sawhorse perch, I bundled it up to store in my car.

I sought activities that would take the edge off Ichabod's ongoing aggressive mood. Sometimes a fast game of catch would work. Sometimes I threw her sticks, and the eagle would dig her talons into them over and over, stripping the bark with her beak and breaking the wood into little pieces. I poked swaths of greenery through the chain-link, shrouding her perch with them. She stripped down every branch except those blocking the view of the workers across the field. The noise and bustle seemed to make her nervous, and she flinched at the sound of boards being dropped.

Conductor training had been stressful, and I was proud of my accomplishment in graduating from it. With my "A" card, I was now qualified to run the yard jobs as a foreman or to take charge of a freight train as conductor. The latter was an exciting thought, but daunting. There were so many things that could go wrong, so many rules to observe that, as my trainer was fond of saying, had been "written in blood." A week after graduation, however, I was laid off.

The layoff meant I had more time to spend with Ichabod, but I worried about money as summer crept into fall. Cage construction slowed down with the advent of the rainy season, and it was hard to keep my mood upbeat. I asked O.W.L.'s permission to fly the eagle in the field, but my request was turned down. With fewer construction workers in evidence, Ichabod lost the nervous aggression that had caused her to rip sticks to smithereens, but she was still unpredictable. Many days my instincts screamed at me to be careful around her. Luckily, her appetite remained strong.

I recalled what falconers had told me about not making Ichabod's cage the primary site for her training, since this would increase her territoriality there. When there were no volunteers in the vicinity, I began leashing the eagle and taking her on my glove for short walks outside the cage. Ichabod consistently bated towards the sawhorse if we walked near it, so after a while I avoided that area, walking instead to a place where we could watch planes take off from the Boundary Bay Airport.

My layoff continued. I'd accepted the need for unemployment insurance, but I scheduled every week-day morning for a job search. I checked regularly with the railway to see how close I was to a recall. I'd not only had a taste of a decent regular income but finally found work that I enjoyed, and the frustration of not being able to do it ate away at me. My hopes rose when I received a call from CPR about filling in for some employees on holiday. I eagerly showed up for the rules refresher course and dusted off my striped coveralls. But days later I was laid off again. It was becoming more and more difficult to find the money to drive to O.W. L., but I skimped on other things to scrape together the necessary funds.

17

A CHALLENGE

BALD EAGLES were more numerous in the fall in southern British Columbia. After visiting the northern salmon runs, which started in late summer, the birds followed the salmon south. Local pairs readied their nests in December, and I'd already seen several eagles flying near the highway in Delta with sprays of foliage in their beaks. With the increase in the number of birds in the Lower Mainland came an increase in injuries. One day, a supervisor at O.W.L. informed me that Ichabod's cage was needed because of the influx of eagles. The new bank of cages across the field from her old one was finally ready, and her new home was to be in one of these.

The new cage was rectangular, with the door at one end. It was smaller and lower than Ichabod's previous cage, and it had a gravel floor. With its grey and white walls, it seemed stark and barren. Most of the wire, which started just above my waist height, was covered with lattice. There was a platform immediately beside the door, and at the far end of the rectangle were two perches. The highest perch was fine for the great horned owls that had lived there previously, but it was much too close to the wall for the eagle's big tail. The height of that perch would also allow her to swoop down on me with ease. Soliciting volunteer help, I took the high perch down and set about making the cage as homey as possible. I found a good solid stump with a rough top for the platform. Looking for ways to introduce some green into the greyness, I poked sprays of cedar and fir in here and there.

I pondered the best way to carry the eagle into the strange bank of cages. There were two small doorways to get through: one that led into an enclosed area, then the door to the cage itself. After debating about catching and carrying her, holding her legs as I would those of a wild eagle, I decided to walk her into the new cage on the glove. I began to give Ichabod extra food four days prior to the move, knowing she'd be stressed in the new cage and might not eat right away.

The day of the move, I went first to Ichabod's new cage, double-checking to see that all was in order. As I left, I propped open the cage door to allow for easier entry.

Ichabod came to the glove readily. Rounding the corner, we walked past her old cage for the last time. I looked in through the chain-link, seeing the empty perches and the well-used stump on the platform. I couldn't help but feel a pang at the change. Ichabod had her mind on other things. She leaned forward as we walked, her eyes scanning the field. When we got within twenty feet of her sawhorse perch, I felt her come to attention, her wings dropping from her body in readiness for flight. "Wait," I commanded. The bird froze, then relaxed, shifting her wings back against her body. As we continued through the grassy corridor at the back of the care centre, we also passed Ichabod's first outdoor cage. Through the chain-link, I could see a juvenile eagle standing on the half wall. Ichabod watched the bird, the crest on the back of her head lifting slightly. The juvenile opened his wings, and I felt an answering tightness course through Ichabod. She leaned against my shoulder to get a better look at the other eagle as we walked by, her beak level with my temple. Her body hummed with tension. Then the juvenile settled his wings, and Ichabod relaxed.

A recently laid gravel road led to Ichabod's new residence. This was unknown territory for us, and the eagle tightened her grip on the glove momentarily. The door to the enclosed area stood before us. Two doorways to go through this time. Whenever I felt Ichabod ready herself to bate, I slowed and spoke to her. She had slicked all her feathers against her body, and she felt light on the glove, as if part of her had already been claimed by the air and the sky.

I paused outside the first door to check that Ichabod's jesses were securely through my glove. The eagle remained still as we stepped inside. Relieved, I moved quickly into the middle of the room. Ahead of us, the second doorway loomed. Ichabod chittered. As she tensed, I spoke quietly and touched my bare finger to her chest, causing her to look down at my hand. Distracting her like this, I stepped into the new cage, pulling the door shut behind us.

Once inside, I slipped the carabiner from the slits at the end of Ichabod's jesses, continuing to hold the leather straps. She stood erect, craning her neck as she sized up the cage. No corner escaped her scrutiny. I walked her to the waist-high perch and said firmly, "Off!" She stepped onto it tentatively. I backed a few steps away and watched as her head turned towards the outside. She was almost directly across the field from her old perch, but her view was blocked by another new cage that was being constructed. As soon as she made her way to the end of her new perch, she would be beside the brambles that shielded the duck pond.

I walked to the platform and placed a rat on the stump. I wasn't thrilled that the platform was so close to the door. Several times, I'd pictured the eagle waiting

there for my entrance, with me unable to see her until
I got inside. Remembering this now, I lifted the rat and
tossed it to the gravel floor midway along the cage.
Ichabod noted the food dropping, then turned back to
peruse the small slice of field she could see. She remained
in that position as I left the cage.

The next day I returned to check on her progress.
Ichabod barely noticed me as I leaned against the closed
door. The rat lay curled where I'd thrown it. The eagle
was absorbed in the comings and goings of three sets of
ducks outside the cage. A pair of green-winged teals flew
by, white bellies flashing bright. A slight breeze lifted
the feathers around Ichabod's chest, but that was the only
movement. As I watched her, I had a craving to feel those
feet holding my arm tightly. I profoundly missed the
sensation of her slamming into the glove. I missed
watching her tail fan just before she landed and seeing
the long primaries separate into distinct "fingers" as she
reached for me. I hoped I'd be able to fly her again soon.

     The following morning I returned with a quail.
Entering Ichabod's cage, I put the still untouched rat
in a bucket, then ripped open the quail's skin, exposing
the breast. Next I jackknifed the legs, splitting the little
bird up the middle. Now that the piece of food looked
so appetizing—at least from an eagle's point of view—
I approached Ichabod with it. I could tell from the white
spray of feces on the wall and ground that she'd been

perched in the same spot for a long time. I looked around for any signs of movement. A small amount of feces stained the wood of the platform to the side of the stump, and I felt an easing in my chest as I noticed it. At least she had stood on the platform, however briefly.

I continued towards Ichabod, stopping a short distance from her. I turned my back and stretched my gloved arm out, the bloody chest of the quail poking from the top of my gloved hand. No reaction. I separated one leg from the quail's body, then stuffed the rest of the bird in my jacket pocket. Clutching the quail leg in my bare hand, I reached for Ichabod's jesses with my gloved hand. She chittered and stepped away. I moved with her, taking a light hold of her jesses. Putting the glove directly in front of her feet, I said, "Up! Up!" She chattered again, then complied, stepping onto the glove in a hesitant manner and standing there using absolutely no grip.

I slipped the quail leg into the palm of my gloved hand, closing my thumb loosely around it. Ichabod looked down. She reached without urgency, grasping the leg in her beak and then swallowing it whole.

"Hallelujah, she eats!" I said to the walls. Before leaving, I set Ichabod on the waist-high perch and draped the rest of the quail over it.

I arrived the next day to see the quail where I'd left it. The eagle stood looking out through the lattice. Discouraged, I sank to the gravel floor by the door and watched

Ichabod. I hated this cage with its drab greyness. Ichabod herself looked dull here. I rose and walked towards her. As I closed in, I raised no glove, instead keeping my arms at my side. Ichabod looked at my face for a long moment, then turned to track another pair of ducks as they flew by, water dropping like diamonds from their legs.

I picked up the quail, ripping its other leg off. Meat gleamed wetly at the edge of bone. I positioned myself about two feet from the eagle, then raised the leg towards her. Turning her head sideways, Ichabod delicately extracted the leg from my fingers, hard shell of beak brushing my fingers like moth wings. I moved the rest of the quail closer to her, then headed for the doorway. Before leaving, I was rewarded with the sight of Ichabod pulling a strip of breast meat from the bird. The eagle's intake of food returned to normal over the next few days, though she didn't exhibit the vibrant personality I had grown to expect.

A month into summer, I was called back to the railway. It was more than four months since I'd worked a shift. I was rusty, but after a few days I began again to speak the language of railcar lengths, knuckles—metal "fists" that joined railcars together—authorizations and air brakes.

Because of a staff shortage, I got to work as a conductor in charge of my first grain train through the Fraser Canyon. As the train clung to the canyon walls,

I watched the river from the best sightseeing seat possible, enthralled with its churning power. The engineman pointed out a giant tree wedged into a cracked rock midstream. It had stuck there in high waters a few years back. The conductors and enginemen were placing bets on when the water would rise high enough again to take the tree from its roost.

Far above the canyon walls, an eagle soared. I blinked, and the bird disappeared. I wondered if I had conjured up its presence in this fantastic setting. I slid the heavy side window open with both hands, half-standing to brace myself. The cab was filled with the sound of rushing water. Ahead of us a tunnel appeared, and as we wound towards it on two thin ribbons of steel, I marvelled at how narrow it was, perfectly carved out in the shape of an engine. The rocks seemed inches from my window as we whisked through.

I also worked switchers, the trains that serviced the waterfront industries. We'd remove empty railcars and replace them with loads or vice versa, often working through the night hours. The other rail employees greeted me as if I'd been gone only a few weeks rather than a few seasons. There were just a handful of women working there, and I worked one shift with Terry Spring's sister, Lorie, as the foreman, me as the brakeman.

I was getting a real taste of work on the railway, and I enjoyed every minute. But five weeks after I had started,

I was again laid off. Despondency filled me. Everything seemed bleak. Ichabod wasn't herself. I didn't like living with so many roommates. Although CPR promised to call me back, I was tired of the layoffs and the consequent living hand-to-mouth. I'd heard of a small outfit that switched intermodal railcars at a port in Delta. I set up a meeting with the manager. Though he usually hired only experienced people, he agreed to let me accompany his best yard foremen to see what I thought. After several shifts to familiarize myself, I was hired as a yard foreman too.

Though the work was part-time, I was finally employed on a regular basis with a railway. The other employees were welcoming, and slowly I gained experience. The railway was located on Roberts Bank, a spit of land made of fill from the ocean floor. The company I worked for provided the container-port longshoremen with loaded or empty railcars, depending on their needs. It was a whole new world for me.

Ichabod was eating, but she was listless. I still wasn't allowed to fly her, and her new cage was more confining than her old one. How could I train her? My agenda had been derailed. Ichabod and I were in limbo, and it made me anxious. My requests for a new flying space seemed to fall on deaf ears. One day I noticed the ground being prepared for more cages. Where and when would I fly her again?

My answer came a short time later. A director informed me that, because the centre still couldn't see how Ichabod would fit into their educational program, I would have to move the eagle somewhere else. I was flummoxed. Where would I take the bird? More importantly, would Fish and Wildlife authorities even allow me to move her? How would I, as an individual, get a permit to keep an eagle?

I called one of the conservation officers I knew at the branch, but it was already past office hours. That evening I phoned Terry to kick around options. As we talked, I realized that Ichabod's life was in jeopardy. The authorities had the right to demand that she be euthanized. Alternatively, she could be sent from O.W.L. to a company that procured animals for use in films. Most of the creatures that seemed happy in that kind of work had been at it from a young age. I couldn't picture Ichabod, who had trouble adjusting to a new cage and who hated her pool to be moved, in the bustling, dynamic atmosphere of a film set. I hung up the phone, my mind swirling with "what if"s. It was up to me to save her. It didn't matter if it hadn't been done before: I had to move the eagle into a situation that suited her.

18

A NEW HOME

F OR THE NEXT few days, I wracked
my brain about where I might take
the eagle. At last I thought of an idea. Years earlier, I'd
worked briefly at an aviary while the head bird caretaker
took a holiday. The Hancock Wildlife Research Aviary
was a breeding centre for many species of exotic birds, as
well as several species of grouse. I'd been impressed with
the aviary's many outdoor pens; most had live trees
growing to the netted roofs.

David Hancock, the aviary's owner, was also a biologist and a writer who operated a small publishing house.
He'd published many books on falconry and exotic

birds. Even better, he had written a book about eagles
and studied the nesting habits of bald eagles. I decided to
approach him about moving Ichabod to one of his pens.

I dropped by the aviary that afternoon. At the top
of a flight of steep wooden stairs, I opened a door into a
long room lined with books. I didn't see the man at the
desk until I heard him laugh and saw him lean back,
running his hand through silvery hair as he spoke ani-
matedly on the phone.

David waved me to a chair as he finished his conversation. Once he had hung up, he turned to me. Nervous,
I blurted out that I needed a place to keep a bald eagle.
David already knew of my involvement at O.W. L., and
though he raised his eyebrows at my request, he seemed
receptive. I found myself telling him of Ichabod's flights
to my glove and of the interruption in our training. As I
wound down, he looked me straight in the eye, and I knew
that he would let me keep the eagle there. After a minute,
he stood up and said, "Let's go look at empty pens."

From a central outdoor aisleway lined with pens, more
aisles branched off on either side. David gave me a choice
of three cages for Ichabod's new home. One of them was
the largest pen on the property. I chose that one. Now
I had a place for the eagle. First step accomplished.

Fish and Wildlife was the next big hurdle. As I drove
home, I played different scenarios in my head. My mind
kept returning to the same groove: "What if they say

no?" My throat tightened as I thought about my life without Ichabod, this vibrant, cantankerous, regal, dangerous creature. I remembered the eagle flying towards me, then stopping halfway to have a bath in a particularly inviting puddle. I pictured her hopping through the grass after a grasshopper. I could almost feel the powerful embrace of her feet around my forearm and the excitement of holding the hissing spitfire that was an eagle in yarak. If there was any way to stay close to this amazing bird, I must try my best to make it happen.

Once home, with Moon Dog leaning against my leg, I called the conservation officer at the ministry. After identifying myself, I paused for a moment, searching for the right words. The officer surprised me by saying he was aware of the situation with the eagle and asking whether I had a place to move her to, at least temporarily. By the time we hung up, I had permission to move the eagle to Hancock's.

Vastly relieved, I began planning for the move, beginning with another trip to the aviary. The pen I had chosen was rectangular in shape, thirty feet by fifty, with live cedar trees growing in the border between the covered and open areas and along the back wall. High-strength net anchored by wood covered the walls and sides of the cage. Giant logs supported by wire hung from the ceiling. These were too close to the top of the cage for an eagle, and I noted all of the other changes needed to make this enclosure habitable for Ichabod. Some of the existing perches were too thin, and their profusion, along with the trees in the cage, made the flying room too limited for a bird with the wingspan of an eagle. The holes in the net roof were big enough to allow the eagle's talons to slip easily in and out, but the side netting was more tightly woven. Ichabod might get snagged in that if she grabbed at the net.

Three friends and I worked to customize the cage, removing perches and framing the sides with wood and lattice. David Hancock kindly provided some of the lumber. It took us three days, spaced out over three weekends, to complete the work.

I surveyed the final product with satisfaction. The fawn-coloured lattice allowed the light through and covered the walls of the cage in pleasing geometrics. More colour came from the deep green of the cedars and the dense silvery twigs of some deciduous trees not yet in leaf. As spring progressed, the cage would be further adorned with green. The ground was a mixture of moss, small shrubs and sand. The roof of the first quarter of the cage was covered with corrugated plastic, and the remainder was open to the sky under net. The highest perch spanned the cage's width, and its roughness and circumference were perfect for an eagle's feet. A chest-high perch supported by notches in two tall logs ran lengthwise in the outdoor area. I'd placed another perch under cover at the far end of the rectangle, as far from the door as possible. A sawhorse with a branch nailed to the top stood fifteen feet from the door, and a large square post was set deep in the sand six feet away. I planned to stand with my back against that when calling Ichabod to the glove. I placed the largest plastic wading pool I could find just out of feces' range of the perch that would get the most sun.

The strange hooting calls of fruit-eating birds called touracos filled the air around me. The touracos were in trailers at this time of year, but I looked forward to seeing the jewel-coloured birds outside in the sun when the days grew warm enough.

A trailer that housed some of the exotic birds also contained a fridge and a small freezer. I would be able to keep Ichabod's food in the freezer and thaw it in the fridge. A bigger freezer in another trailer could also be used to store large quantities of frozen food. I called someone I knew who bred rats and placed an order. There was a quail breeder living fifteen minutes from Hancock's, and I thought about purchasing some freshly killed quail to add to the bounty in the freezer. After reviewing my finances, however, I decided to wait. I planned to feed Ichabod food that was as fresh as possible, so I bought only small quantities for storage. Finally, after buying a vitamin supplement known to be excellent for raptors, I was prepared. Two months after being told to move the eagle, it was time to arrange the move.

I ASKED TERRY to help me move Ichabod, since his old truck would hold the large kennel cab we needed. A roadway ran alongside the eagle's cage at O.W. L., allowing us to drive right up beside it. In preparation, I had placed a snug-fitting piece of carpet on the bottom of the kennel cab, and over that a thin towel. The wire along the sides and front was covered with cardboard, with holes punched here and there to allow for easy breathing. Many of the larger kennel cabs were set up this way. It kept the occupant quiet, doing away with the need to cover the cab with a sheet.

Terry and I had decided to catch Ichabod in her cage and carry her to the kennel cab, to save us manoeuvring the big crate through the doorway with the eagle inside. As I placed the empty cab on the tailgate of the truck, I heard the *pshew* call of a red-tailed hawk. Against the faint clouds mixed with pale blue overhead, I caught sight of the bird. It spun a weave of wide circles, revealing, by its path, the invisible rising thermals of air over the farmer's field beside us. Lucy, the red-tailed hawk, answered the soaring stranger with a haunting *keerrr,* followed by a series of short yips and whines. The wild red-tail remained silent, but the bird seemed to shift its direction, slipping onto a rising column of air that would take it closer to Lucy's cage.

Since beginning to train Ichabod, I'd pushed rehab work with the other birds to the periphery of my mind, feeling only the occasional stab of jealous curiosity when I saw a new patient enter the care centre in the arms of a volunteer. Rehab was work I loved and had a knack for. As I stood under the bright March sky, I realized how much I would miss it. Terry and I turned our attention to the capture of Ichabod. As we'd arranged in the past when changing her jesses, Terry would net the eagle and contain her in his gloved hands; I'd sneak in quietly from behind and slip the hood on.

Terry walked into Ichabod's cage holding the net in front of him. I held the door ajar with my foot. I winced when I saw Ichabod's fear of the net, but I knew this was the quickest, safest method for containing her. The last few times I'd held her legs out for Terry to jess after the netting, Ichabod had relaxed at my soothing words, her head under my chin, her back against my chest and stomach.

Terry was fast with the net. Ichabod lifted off her perch, but he scooped her before she'd travelled three feet, bringing her to the ground carefully. I made my way around behind her as Terry took hold of her legs and extricated her grasping talons from the net.

As I grabbed Ichabod's head from behind, her yellow eyes met mine for a second. I winced again, but my hand moved deftly, sliding the hood over her face so that her beak protruded comfortably from the opening and her eyes were covered by the brown leather. She ceased her struggles immediately. Dennis, the local falconer who'd made the hood, had painted an eagle on top, and from above I looked down on the miniature bird with its white head and outstretched wings. I tightened the traces so that the hood cupped the back of Ichabod's head snugly.

I lifted the eagle clear of the net and the ground, carefully tucking her wings around her. I carried her almost upright, because I knew most birds were more comfortable that way. With her brilliant eyes covered, Ichabod seemed more like a package of feathers with a heartbeat than a sentient being.

I walked carefully out of the cage towards the truck. Once we were there, I swung Ichabod around to face away from me, setting her feet on the towel in the middle of the crate. She wobbled slightly, unsure of her bearings with her eyes covered. As soon as she stood steadily, I released her and shut the door, making sure the spring-loaded catch was secure. I opened the gates leading from the back of the property and watched as Terry drove Ichabod from the home she'd known for seven years. I would follow them in my car.

At Hancock's, Terry and I manoeuvred the crate into the outdoor aisleway, then turned into another aisle after a few paces. The first cage on the left was Ichabod's. We carried the crate through the narrow doorway awkwardly, Terry slipping through first. Once we had set the crate on the sand a few feet from the door, Terry closed the cage door behind us. Crouching, I pinched the catch on the kennel cab and reached in with my bare hands for Ichabod's jesses. I unsnarled one easily from under her foot, but I had to give her a gentle nudge to dislodge the other. The hooded eagle chittered uncertainly, then reached out for an imaginary glove. I moved my hand away smartly, and she placed her foot back on the towel. I closed the crate door momentarily, pulling the glove onto my left hand. My flesh-and-blood fingers curved into the stiffened leather ones. Inside my stomach, butterflies fluttered.

I pressed my gloved forearm against Ichabod's legs. "Up! Up!" I commanded. Ichabod stepped onto the glove, and I lifted her free of the crate. I slipped the jesses securely through my gloved fingers, deciding to forgo the leash. She gripped slightly with the motion, then stood relaxed. Terry loosened the drawstrings and slid the hood forward off her head.

Ichabod blinked, and her pupils shrank. Her head feathers, depressed in an avian version of "hat head," first lifted, then slicked back against the bones of her skull, making her beak look huge and ungainly. The next instant she puffed up the back of her head into a headdress. She craned her neck sideways, then all around, evaluating her new surroundings. A touraco whooped from inside a nearby trailer. Ichabod startled, dropping her wings as if to bate. But before I could reassure her, she settled.

With Ichabod still on the glove, I walked a few steps closer to the cage's sawhorse perch. I lowered her slightly and opened my gloved fingers to free the jesses. "Off!" She leapt and landed, rocking the sawhorse. She'd barely touched down when she opened her wings and flew in a straight line for a higher perch. After a moment there, her wings unfolded, and she flew towards the long branch supported by notched logs. Seconds later, she was in the air again, heading for the highest perch in the cage. Having done a complete circuit, she settled herself, flicking her tail fussily from side to side.

Before leaving the cage, I put a medium-sized rat on the ground near the high perch. I took one more satisfied look at Ichabod standing tall on the branch, her head twisting and craning to take in her surroundings. As I drove home, I wondered what she'd make of all the strange new sounds. Luckily, Hancock's was less than ten minutes by car from my house. I could visit the eagle every day and spend more time with her than ever before.

By the next morning, rain had turned Hancock's aviary into a dripping, mist-shrouded forest. The outdoor cages were mostly vacant at this time of year because of the cold temperatures, and I had a sense of the plants taking over. Many of the trees were budding, and some had already unfurled giant spatulate leaves. Beads of wet glistened on the net roofs.

Ichabod stood on the high perch in her cage. The rat

lay soaked and untouched on the sandy ground. I moved it under cover but left it in plain sight of her perch. When I returned on the third day, Ichabod was still on the high perch. I saw no evidence of feces anywhere except underneath her. Rain continued to fall steadily. Despite having the superior waterproofing of a bald eagle, Ichabod was beginning to look damp. Her white head was grey in colour.

I placed a fresh rat under cover ten feet away from Ichabod. The high perch she stood on was not under cover, but two other perches were. I raised one of them to match the height of the outdoor perch. Ichabod showed no interest in it. She stayed where she was, the heavy rain plastering her feathers to her body. I was worried. The last thing I wanted was for her to become ill when her immune system was already compromised from the stress of the move. The strange birds in the other cages concerned me as well—were they prone to diseases that Ichabod could contract?

On the fourth day, I exchanged Ichabod's rat for a fresh one. Still no response. She remained on the high outside perch, her head thrown back, staring through the net at the sky. A noise at ground level would capture her attention briefly, but she always lifted her head again to the rain. I noticed her several times standing on tiptoe, peering around heavy foliage. I figured she had spotted a grouse in the neighbouring pen.

Four days had passed, and Ichabod still hadn't eaten. During her past episodes of "fasting," the eagle had eaten when she was ready. But because the change had been more dramatic this time, I felt I had greater cause for concern. There were more than two hundred birds on this property, and the area was damp and heavily vegetated. Darkness came fast under the trees, and several times, driving in from the open road after working a day shift, I was shocked to see how dark it already was in the cages. The occasional *psst* of a barn owl hit my ears at dusk, but I seldom saw the ghostly bird. In the evenings, owls would call in the large trees.

The light was dimming as I entered Ichabod's cage on the fifth day. Instead of stopping close to her and talking as I usually did, I walked under her high perch, a move that would have earned me an attack, or at least a threat, from the old Ichabod. On a whim, I stretched tall and reached towards her feet with my bare hands, hoping to evoke a reaction. The eagle stood as if carved.

The wind had picked up, and it rustled the leaves of trees in the neighbouring cages. Most of the touracos were snug and warm in their trailers, eating their freshly ground fruit. But the giant grouse called capercaillies, native to northern Europe and Asia, moved ponderously around their pen across the covered hallway. A haunting, nasal cry rang out above the sound of the rain. I knew it came from an African hornbill in a trailer nearby, but it had a more distant sound. I felt as if the nearest human was miles and miles away.

The pelting rain plastered my hair to my head as I stood in the cage, face tilted to the sky. The outline of the eagle above me was blurred. I again reached for her feet. She inclined her head towards me and shook herself, then moved sideways on the perch, away from me. I stood for another minute, my outstretched hand floating in the grey light like a pale starfish.

I lowered my arm, feeling foolish. Ichabod again looked down at me, and her eyes seemed dull. Suddenly I was angry: angry at having to move her, angry at the falconers for telling me she'd eat when she was hungry, angry at how perilously low my funds were after revamping the cage, angry at myself for continually living with my nerve endings on the outside of my skin.

When I was done finding things to be angry about, I left the cage and sat on a stool in the hallway. I could see Ichabod's yellow feet and ankles, a brown leg and part of a wing—the sweep of feather just as it started to curve back towards her tail. I wasn't sure what to do, and for the moment, I felt depleted.

The next day, I bought thirty freshly killed quail from the local breeder. I put the bulk of them in the large freezer, keeping out five to add to the store of rats in the small freezer. I took one to use immediately.

Holding the quail by the feet, I headed for Ichabod's

cage. The dead bird hung from my hand, its breast heavy, the tiny talons on its toes scratching my palm. The dark roving eye of a touraco across the aisle watched my progress. Today the weather had warmed enough to allow some of the fruit-eaters to leave their heated trailer through a door propped open into a netted pen. The stiff comb of black feathers on the touraco's head and the strange orange markings around his eyes gave him a manic look. I thought, not for the first time, that touracos were the strangest of all birds. They bounded from perch to perch, barely unfurling their wings but still revealing flashes of blood-red feathers. They were given to sudden bouts of communal whooping: one touraco would start, and every touraco on the property would join in in a cacophony of sound. I wondered what Ichabod made of the unusual racket.

I unlocked Ichabod's cage and stepped inside. Ripping a leg, complete with meaty thigh, from the quail's body, I lifted it towards her perch. The sky was bright for a change. Because of the light behind her, I couldn't tell that Ichabod's beak had lowered until it touched my fingers. She extracted the quail leg and swallowed it, the bird's pale foot visible in the pink of her opened mouth for a moment.

I threw the rest of the quail to the ground, and Ichabod followed, the wind of her passing brushing my cheek. She hunched over the food, unconcerned that my sneakers depressed the sand only six feet away. Soon, quail bound in one foot, she hobbled towards a large log resting against her pool. She hopped onto it, balanced herself and continued eating.

I took the opportunity to knock down the perch Ichabod had stood on for so long and lower it to waist height. Now the highest perch in the cage was under cover, a roughened branch suspended just above my head. It was well back from the doorway and from the support post that I intended to use as protection when I called Ichabod to the glove. I wouldn't do that right away, though. I decided to give the eagle more time to settle in before beginning our training again.

19

CLOSE QUARTERS

DURING THE WEEKS that followed,
I left food in the cage for Ichabod
every day. Once she had shown a consistently healthy
appetite, I decided it was time to offer her food on the
glove again. But although she would step onto my gloved
arm from the perch if I brushed the glove against her feet,
she was unwilling to fly to it. I changed the frequency of
her feeding to every second day, hoping to sharpen her
interest in eating.

It was a long time since I'd seen the vibrant creature
that flew to my glove in the field. I longed to see the
spark return to Ichabod's eyes, but her expression

remained blank and distant. I laced her food with small amounts of vitamins formulated for birds of prey, and once a week I fed her a larger quantity of them. Despite her lacklustre reactions to me, her feathers took on a gloss they'd never shown before.

Although I was worried about Ichabod, I enjoyed my work at Roberts Bank. The wind never stopped blowing there. At the end of the spit of land, where giant cranes unloaded the ships, it was sometimes strong enough to shut the port down.

My crew consisted of myself, as yard foreman, and a locomotive engineer. We would attach a locomotive to the railcars, then switch the cars around into their order of destination, with the eastern localities on the tail end: Toronto, then the Prairies, and so on, until the resulting train mirrored the country's geographic order. After brake-testing a locomotive, we would join it to the completed train, leaving it ready for its crew to take it eastwards.

At night, with the engineer sometimes six thousand feet away on his locomotive, I was alone in the rail yard. Barn owls flitted overhead, making their otherworldly screeches, and several times I surprised a great horned owl perching on a metal container that had been loaded onto a railcar. During the day, I watched flocks of shore-birds swirl and turn, breasts flashing silver in the sun. A peregrine falcon occasionally perched on the power

poles. And the high-pitched bickering of bald eagles
never failed to turn my head. One day my engineer and
I counted ten eagles on the poles along the road.

I visited Ichabod as often as I could, always at least
four times a week. She seemed settled in her new home
now, no longer startling when a neighbour's donkey
brayed or when the Impeyan pheasant, feathered a deep
iridescent blue, dropped from his perch in the pen at the
end of the hall and stalked down his long narrow runway.

One afternoon as I parked in the shadowy lot at Hancock's I noticed broken branches littering the ground.
A wind storm, I guessed. I wondered how Ichabod's cage
had stood up to it. I collected her food, shrugged on a
light jacket and hurried down the aisle, the glove bent
over my arm.

From the outside, it was difficult to tell if the roof
netting of Ichabod's cage was still intact. The big leaves
of a young maple tree blocked my sightline. I peered
through the lattice that covered the door. The parts of the
roof I could see from there looked fine. But I couldn't
see the eagle.

With a sinking feeling, I unlocked the cage door
and slipped the glove onto my arm. But before I could
pull the door open, a rustle at ground level caught my
attention. Ichabod stood in the sand peering up at me. I
was relieved but surprised. I'd never seen her in this location. Still outside the door, I crouched down until her

head was level with my knees. She reached with her beak through the lattice. My right hand moved instinctively to touch her, as you might an animal at a petting zoo. I hesitated once I realized what I was doing, then continued, lulled by the soft look of Ichabod's eyes. The hard shell was warm under my finger. The hooked tip of her beak was pale, almost transparent; the smooth downcurve above the tip was a deeper yellow. After a moment, Ichabod withdrew her head. She hopped away from the door, lifting herself onto the sawhorse perch with one lazy flap. She watched me from there as I entered the cage.

I took two long strides to the post. From there, ritual movements flowed through my body: turn sideways to the eagle, reach into my pocket for the rat piece, twist so my back faced the bird, straighten my gloved arm, sling the rat through my fingers.

"Up! Up!" For a moment, nothing happened. Then, suddenly, the eagle was in the air. I felt something break loose in my chest, as if I was drawing air into my body for the first time in a long time. Her feet landed wide and sure on the glove.

In the days that followed, Ichabod flew to the glove like an old pro. She began to seem like her old self in other ways, too. She cried her challenge to people feeding the other birds, throwing back her head and holding her wings out to flap only the very tips. In short order, I taught her to fly to the sawhorse perch in the cage, then

fly up to my glove from there. From that angle, I was
able to keep the post safely against the back of my head.

Soon I began working on getting Ichabod through
the doorway of her cage. This door was the least inviting
one we had ever tackled. The concrete floor of the narrow
hallway was higher than the sandy ground of the cage,
so I would have to take a step up to get to it. The hallway
was roofed with corrugated plastic. To get to the mesh-
covered door that led to the wide outdoor aisleway,
I would have to make a sharp right turn once we were
in the hall. The aisleway itself was roofed in net.

The first time I tried it, Ichabod took one look into
the narrow hallway and leapt from my glove back into her
cage. I began the process of feeding her near the door, but
we made little progress. One afternoon, I got the idea of
enticing her into the hallway on her own steam. I placed
a plump quail on the concrete and propped open the cage
door. Ichabod, already waiting by the door, shocked me
by leaping onto the quail without a moment's hesitation.
I stumbled out of the way as a wing struck my leg. One
taloned foot curled around the meat, and the other
grabbed my sneaker. "Hey!" I yelled. Ichabod lowered
her head, peered at her prizes and crowed triumphantly.

I slowly tried to move my foot and was rewarded with
tightened talons. An impasse. The eagle turned her head
sideways and looked up at me, her visible eye glittering.
Without warning, she unfurled her wings and leapt for

the cage clutching both the quail and my foot, unwilling
to let go of either. Taken by surprise, I slipped and fell
onto my tailbone. I saw stars for a moment. When my
vision cleared, I was sitting on the concrete with my legs
stretched into the cage. The eagle was gripping higher up
my foot now, near the ankle. I could feel that the talons
had pierced the skin near my anklebone. Though my face
was still higher than hers, I was uncomfortably aware of
my vulnerability.

Ichabod lifted her beak and stared at me with an
expression that, in a human, could only be called malig-
nant. I bent my free leg slowly, bringing the foot towards
me in readiness. I might have to try to stand quickly. My
spine ached, and I could feel the pain all the way up my
neck. "And I wanted you back to your old self," I muttered. As if in response, Ichabod tightened her grip.
Then she looked down at the foot still holding the quail.
Maybe she was getting hungry, I thought. Almost delicately, Ichabod extracted her talons from my ankle and
hobbled awkwardly away, one foot raised by the quail
it grasped. I stood gingerly, my spine clicking like casta-
nets. Blood stained my sock. I looked into the cage as I
closed the door. Ichabod was balanced over her food,
talons from each foot steadying it, beak ripping away
large chunks. "Welcome home," I said wryly. The eagle
didn't acknowledge me as she proceeded to demolish
her quail with gusto.

20

A FEATHER'S MESSAGE

SPRING TURNED into summer, then fall. Ichabod seemed content in her new home, and I went there to work with her as often as I could. Our training progressed slowly, but by September she was accustomed to standing on my gloved arm while I walked through the doorway out of her cage. We had started going for short walks again, strolling alongside the other cages in the aisleway.

Early one overcast morning I jumped in my car and headed for the aviary, intending to make a quick visit. As I approached Ichabod's cage I blew a short blast on my whistle, expecting to hear the telltale thump as she left her perch and the sound of her wings cutting through air. But I heard nothing. Opening the door to her cage, I saw her standing on the ground not far from her sawhorse. It was an odd place for her to be. I stepped closer, and my stomach contracted. The eagle's eyes looked dull. I bent and offered her the glove, my breath trapped in my chest. She stepped on easily. I lifted her, and she half opened her wings in response, as she always did. But when she turned her head towards the door and opened her beak to call, a bright stream of blood spattered from her mouth onto my sweatshirt.

Though I moved fast after that, I seemed to be in a dreamlike state. One of Hancock's staffpeople helped me whisk the eagle into a crate and load the crate into my car. As I drove, I called the vet that O.W.L. used from my cell phone, knowing that regular vets lacked the knowledge and often the desire to work with raptors. I picked up a friend on the way for emotional support.

At the clinic, I held Ichabod for X-rays as I had so many eagles in the past. I tried to be calm and professional, but my tears wouldn't stop. The X-rays showed large masses in both her lungs, and the vet believed that one of the masses had burst. My friend, who worked as an emergency-room nurse, asked the questions I couldn't seem to form with my numb lips. The situation looked extremely serious, the vet said, and there was really nothing he could do. Ichabod was back in the crate now, standing a little more strongly on her legs. The clinic gave me some rehydration fluids for her and sent us home.

Back at Hancock's, I carried Ichabod's crate to the heated food-preparation trailer. I could see Ichabod inside, her head hanging. I knelt on the floor and, with shaking hands, pressed the catch on the crate and opened the door. The eagle lifted her head and stepped forward, putting one huge foot onto my lap and then the other. Her head dropped again, and I knelt with her against my chest. She coughed, spewing blood over my jeans. I could hardly see for tears. I turned her around gently and placed her back on the blanket in the cage. I shut the door and called again for help. At a small animal clinic just down the road, I held Ichabod while the vet administered a lethal injection.

A LONG TIME PASSED before I could enjoy the sight of an eagle again. I made myself watch them fly anyway, hoping to heal. About nine months after Ichabod's death, I took a new job with B.C. Rail. Their freight and passenger trains travelled through some of the most stunning scenery I had ever seen. Riding from North Vancouver along Howe Sound and through Squamish, I was always reminded of the eagle count I had participated in years earlier. The train passed through Whistler, Pemberton and several rural communities before skimming along Anderson and Seton Lakes on a tiny shelf between steep mountain and water.

On a passenger train one day, I stood beside the locomotive engineer. We slipped around the sharp curves beside Seton Lake, sand-coloured rock climbing steeply on one side. I bent my knees to peer up at the rock face, looking for white specks that could indicate mountain goats. As I straightened, I caught movement out of the corner of one eye. Flying beside my engineer's window was an adult bald eagle. I drank in the deep wing beats, the dark feathers outlined crisply against the blue. The bird was large; a female, I guessed. I watched her yellow eyes, waiting to see if she would look our way. Ahead of us a bare-branched tree, the only one in sight, grew crookedly towards the water. I knew the eagle would land there. Transfixed, I took in what I had seen so many times before: her tail fanning and dropping, her wings folding dramatically forward as she slowed. As her yellow feet swung forward, I could almost feel them on my glove. I caught a glimpse of her toes grasping the branch, and then we flashed past. In my mind, I could see the settling of wings over her back, the whisk of her tail from side to side as she subsided. I waited for sadness to come, but all I felt was a kind of peace. That, and a thankfulness for the great gift Ichabod had given me.

Later that week, I stood in the horse field behind my house, watching as a big bay leapt and wheeled, scarring

the earth with his hooves. His companion, a roan year-
ling, followed suit. Though they were at least twenty feet
from me, I felt I was in the midst of the action. The bay
thundered past. He looked curiously light on his feet, but
I could feel the ground vibrate. The world seemed filled
with horses and their sounds, the gritty pound of hooves
and the rhythmical whoosh of air from their lungs.

As the bay slid to a stop, ribs heaving like bellows,
I saw something twirling in the air. It landed gently on
the grass. Curious, I walked towards it. When I drew
closer, I was astounded to see the sceptrelike shape of a
large eagle feather. I looked to the sky quickly, but the
arch of blue was clear of wings.

The feather lifted, then settled, only to twitch almost
into flight again. I stooped to retrieve it, grateful and
awed. It was a sign I couldn't ignore: whatever might
happen from here, my destiny was inextricably entwined
with eagles.

ACKNOWLEDGEMENTS

FIRST, I WANT to acknowledge the love and support of my mom, Joyce; my dad, Jack; my sister, Shelley; and my brother, Brian. Thanks to my childhood friends from the Prairies, including Jana, Nicole, Renata and Laura. Thanks also to my English teacher at Shaftsbury High School, Mr. Davidson, who first encouraged me to have original thoughts.

My favourite book on bald eagles, of the many I've read over the years, is *The Bald Eagle: Haunts and Habits of a Wilderness Monarch*, by Jon M. Gerrard and Gary R. Bortolotti (Smithsonian Institution Press, 1988). It verified many of my own observations about these wonderful birds and added immeasurably to my knowledge of them.

Thanks to all my friends on the West Coast: Siri, Pam, Jackie, Penelope, Brenda, Claudia, Andrea, Sue, Maria and Jacquelin, to name a few. Special thanks to Lynne Short. Thank you to David Hancock for providing Ichabod's final home. Thanks also to friends and mentors Sandy Shreve, Matt Hughes, Linda Kadlec-Diver, Les Hempsall, Debbie Stasik, Bob Westerholm, Bette Hawes, Peter Mayer, Anne-Marie Steenge and Liz Jurkowski; all of them are writers of great talent who provide tireless encouragement for others.

Thanks to Barbara Pulling, my editor, for her patience and skill, as well as to Rob Sanders of Greystone Books and to Linda McKnight, my agent. Thanks to the Surrey Writers' Conference for the contacts that made this memoir happen.

Finally, thanks to my animal family: Moon Dog and Chay (canine), Ben (equine) and Riley (feline), who kept me company as I wrestled with words and deadlines.

BRENDA COX grew up in Winnipeg, Manitoba. Her reverence for wild places began with her horseback rides through the Assiniboine forest at the edge of the city, where she was thrilled by the owls and hawks she spotted. She studied biology and geography at Simon Fraser University and spent eight years as a volunteer supervisor at a wildlife sanctuary, which is where she met Ichabod, the bald eagle. Brenda Cox currently lives in Aldergrove, B.C., with two dogs, a horse and a cat. Along with writing, she works as a conductor for the railway.